CALEB ROSS

Best API Development Practices For Beginners

Essential Tips to Master API Development from the Ground Up

First edition

This book was professionally typeset on Reedsy.
Find out more at reedsy.com

Contents

Introduction

What Is an API and Why It Matters (2000 words)

What is an API? Application Programming Interfaces (APIs) are the backbone of modern software ecosystems. An API allows different software applications to communicate and interact with each other, exchanging data and functionalities. At its core, an API acts as an intermediary that enables one piece of software to request data or perform functions from another. This communication typically happens over the internet using web protocols such as HTTP.

For example, when you use a mobile app to check the weather, the app sends a request to a weather service API, which processes the request and sends the weather data back to your app. Without APIs, these seamless interactions would require apps to do all the data retrieval and processing on their own, leading to inefficiency and an increased development burden.

Why APIs Matter The role APIs play in modern development cannot be overstated. They allow developers to create applications that are not monolithic but instead composed of services and functionalities provided by third-party systems. This not only speeds up development but also adds value through integrations.

APIs power virtually every aspect of digital life. Social media platforms, payment gateways, mapping services, and even smart devices rely on APIs to deliver functionality. Here are some of the primary reasons APIs are critical:

1. **Seamless Integration**: APIs enable different software systems to work together, whether integrating payment gateways in e-commerce sites or embedding map services in travel apps.
2. **Efficiency and Modularity**: By using APIs, developers can rely on reusable components instead of building everything from scratch. This leads to shorter development times and more focus on core product innovations.
3. **Future-Proofing Applications**: With APIs, systems can evolve independently. A developer can upgrade one part of a system (like a backend service) without affecting how users interact with the application front-end.
4. **Access to External Data and Services**: APIs provide easy access to third-party services. For example, a financial application may integrate with a bank's API to retrieve real-time account information.
5. **Ecosystem Creation**: Major platforms like Google, Facebook, and Amazon provide APIs that other developers use to build on top of their services. This creates a symbiotic relationship where platforms expand through API usage and developers benefit from advanced features.

Types of APIs There are several types of APIs commonly used, and understanding the differences will help developers choose the right approach for specific projects:

- **Web APIs (REST, SOAP, GraphQL)**: Web APIs are the most common and allow applications to communicate over the internet. REST (Representational State Transfer) and SOAP (Simple Object Access Protocol) are two of the most used web service protocols. GraphQL is another modern approach that is becoming popular due to its flexibility in querying data.
- **Operating System APIs**: These APIs allow software to interact with the underlying operating system. For example, the Windows API lets applications communicate with the Windows OS for tasks such as file management, memory allocation, and thread management.
- **Library APIs**: These are APIs provided by libraries or frameworks

within programming languages. For instance, the Java Collections API provides a set of pre-defined functions for handling data structures like lists and maps.

- **Hardware APIs**: These APIs allow software to interact with hardware components. For instance, Android apps use hardware APIs to interact with a smartphone's camera, GPS, or accelerometer.

Use Cases and Industry Examples APIs touch every industry, from finance to healthcare, e-commerce to entertainment. Consider the following examples:

- **Financial Services**: Banks provide APIs for developers to access account information, initiate transactions, and integrate banking services into third-party applications (e.g., PayPal using banking APIs).
- **Social Media**: Social media platforms like Facebook, Twitter, and Instagram provide APIs that allow third-party apps to post content, retrieve user data, and integrate platform features.
- **E-Commerce**: E-commerce sites often use APIs to manage payments (Stripe, PayPal), product inventory, shipping information, and customer data.

APIs are not just beneficial for developers; they are a critical business tool that allows companies to innovate, scale, and maintain a competitive edge. They streamline processes, encourage partnerships, and unlock revenue opportunities through third-party integration.

Understanding the Role of APIs in Modern Software (1500 words)

The role of APIs in modern software is foundational to how applications are built, operate, and evolve. APIs are the bridge between different services, enabling a microservices architecture, which has transformed the way software is structured and delivered.

1. Microservices Architecture In the past, monolithic applications were the standard. All the application's components were tightly coupled in a single, unified system. However, this approach became unwieldy as systems grew in complexity. Enter microservices architecture—a modern approach to building software that divides large applications into smaller, independent services that communicate with each other via APIs.

APIs play a pivotal role in microservices because they are the mechanism by which services communicate. Each microservice is developed, deployed, and scaled independently, and the API provides a standard interface for interaction. This approach allows for more agile development, continuous integration, and rapid scaling.

2. Cloud Computing and APIs Cloud platforms such as Amazon Web Services (AWS), Google Cloud, and Microsoft Azure are built on APIs. These cloud providers expose APIs that developers use to interact with their services, including computing power, storage, and databases. For example, a company can use AWS APIs to automatically scale their server capacity based on user demand.

By leveraging cloud APIs, developers can build highly scalable and resilient applications without managing underlying infrastructure. This "API-first" approach enables applications to be more flexible, reducing time-to-market and increasing responsiveness to changes.

3. Mobile Applications and APIs Mobile applications are inherently dependent on APIs to function. Whether it's a weather app fetching forecast data or a social media app pulling in posts, APIs are at the core of mobile development. With APIs, mobile apps can offload complex tasks (e.g., data storage, processing) to backend services, keeping the app lightweight and responsive.

For example, Uber's mobile app uses a variety of APIs for different functions:

- Mapping and location services (Google Maps API)
- Payment processing (Stripe API)
- User authentication (OAuth API)

This multi-API approach makes the app feature-rich while keeping the user experience seamless.

4. APIs and the Internet of Things (IoT) The Internet of Things (IoT) is rapidly growing, connecting devices from smart thermostats to fitness trackers. APIs are critical in enabling these devices to communicate with cloud services and other devices. IoT devices send data via APIs to central servers, which can process the data and send back commands (e.g., turning on lights, adjusting temperatures).

For example, a smart home system might use an API to integrate with a smart thermostat, allowing the user to control it remotely via an app or even set up automated temperature adjustments.

5. Enterprise Software and APIs Enterprise applications, such as CRM (Customer Relationship Management) systems, ERPs (Enterprise Resource Planning), and HR management systems, rely on APIs for integration across departments. For example, Salesforce provides an API that allows developers to connect the CRM to other enterprise tools, ensuring data consistency and streamlined workflows.

6. APIs and AI/ML Integration APIs have become crucial in enabling AI and machine learning models to integrate with other systems. AI platforms like TensorFlow or OpenAI provide APIs that allow applications to request predictions, analyses, or even process language queries. This allows non-expert developers to incorporate cutting-edge AI into their applications with minimal effort.

For example, a chatbot can use an AI-powered language processing API to understand user queries and provide human-like responses, enhancing customer support.

The Beginner's Roadmap to API Development (2000 words)

For beginners, diving into API development may seem daunting, but with the right roadmap, it can be a smooth journey. This section outlines a beginner-friendly approach to API development, guiding through the key stages.

1. Start with the Basics: Learn HTTP and REST Understanding HTTP

(Hypertext Transfer Protocol) is the foundation of API development. HTTP is the protocol used for communication between a client (e.g., browser, mobile app) and a server. Key concepts to master include:

- **HTTP Methods**: GET (retrieve data), POST (send data), PUT (update data), DELETE (remove data).
- **Status Codes**: 200 (OK), 404 (Not Found), 500 (Server Error), etc.
- **Headers**: Used to pass metadata about the request and response.

Most modern APIs are RESTful APIs. REST (Representational State Transfer) is an architectural style that allows stateless communication between client and server using standard HTTP methods. For a beginner, understanding the principles of REST is critical. REST APIs are simple to design and consume, making them a great starting point.

2. Choose a Programming Language and Framework Once you've mastered the basics of HTTP and REST, the next step is to choose a programming language and framework. Beginners should choose languages that offer robust API development frameworks:

- **JavaScript**: Use Node.js with Express.js to build APIs.
- **Python**: Flask or Django are powerful for API development.
- **Java**: Spring Boot is a popular choice for building robust APIs.
- **C#**: ASP.NET Core is an excellent choice for developing scalable APIs.

Pick one language that resonates with your existing knowledge or preferences and stick to it until you become proficient.

3. Set Up Your Development Environment Install the necessary software tools for building APIs:

- **Code Editor**: Choose an editor like Visual Studio Code, Sublime Text, or PyCharm.
- **API Testing Tool**: Postman or Insomnia are excellent tools to test API endpoints and see responses in real-time.

- **Version Control**: Git is essential for managing code and collaborating with others.

4. Build Your First Simple API Start small by building a simple API that handles basic CRUD operations (Create, Read, Update, Delete). For example, create a "to-do" list API where users can add, delete, or update tasks.
Here's an outline of steps to build a simple to-do list API:

1. **Set up a project** using your chosen framework.
2. **Define endpoints** for creating, reading, updating, and deleting tasks.
3. **Connect to a database** (SQLite or MongoDB for simplicity).
4. **Test the API** using Postman or curl.
5. **Deploy the API** locally to see it work in action.

5. Understand Data Formats (JSON vs. XML) APIs communicate using data formats like JSON (JavaScript Object Notation) or XML (eXtensible Markup Language). JSON has become the de facto standard due to its simplicity and ease of use with modern web technologies. Ensure you understand how to:

- Parse JSON data in your programming language.
- Send and receive data in the appropriate format.

6. Learn API Security Basics Security is a critical aspect of API development, even for beginners. Learn about basic authentication mechanisms:

- **API Keys**: A simple method to authenticate users by including a key in API requests.
- **OAuth2**: A more advanced, token-based authentication system used by many modern APIs.

7. Study API Documentation Reading and understanding API documentation is a crucial skill. Many developers fail to realize that good documentation is essential for API usability. Practice writing concise, clear documentation for your APIs and using Swagger to auto-generate docs.

8. Test Your API Extensively Testing is vital in ensuring your API works correctly across different conditions. Learn how to write unit tests for your endpoints and use API testing tools to simulate various scenarios.

9. Deploy Your API Once your API is working locally, learn how to deploy it to a cloud platform like Heroku or AWS. Deployment teaches you how to manage real-world issues like scaling and performance optimization.

Key Technologies and Tools You'll Need (1500 words)

Building APIs requires a solid set of technologies and tools. Here's what you'll need to get started:

1. Programming Language and Frameworks Your choice of programming language dictates the frameworks you use for API development. Some popular combinations include:

- **JavaScript + Node.js + Express.js**: For building fast, scalable APIs in JavaScript.
- **Python + Flask/Django**: Python's frameworks are great for rapid API development.
- **Java + Spring Boot**: For enterprise-level API development.
- **C# + ASP.NET Core**: A highly scalable solution for API development on Microsoft's .NET platform.

2. Databases APIs often need to interact with databases to store and retrieve data. Beginners should familiarize themselves with:

- **SQL Databases**: MySQL, PostgreSQL, SQLite.
- **NoSQL Databases**: MongoDB, Firebase (for JSON storage).

3. API Testing Tools Testing is crucial for ensuring API reliability. Use tools like:

- **Postman**: Widely used for testing API endpoints and sending requests.
- **Insomnia**: A simple, open-source API client.
- **Swagger**: Not only for documentation but also for testing APIs via its built-in UI.

4. Source Control and Collaboration Using Git for version control is essential when working on API projects. Tools like GitHub or GitLab help with:

- **Source Control**: Tracking code changes and collaborating with other developers.
- **CI/CD Integration**: Automatically testing and deploying code changes.

5. Cloud Platforms for API Deployment Cloud platforms enable you to deploy and scale APIs. Popular choices include:

- **AWS (Amazon Web Services)**: Offers scalable infrastructure for hosting APIs.
- **Heroku**: A simple platform for deploying smaller projects.
- **Google Cloud Platform (GCP)**: Provides APIs for everything from AI to storage.
- **Azure**: Microsoft's cloud platform offers excellent services for hosting ASP.NET Core APIs.

6. Logging and Monitoring Tools Once your API is live, you'll need tools to monitor its performance and troubleshoot issues:

- **Loggly**: Aggregates and monitors logs for easy debugging.
- **New Relic**: Provides insights into API performance and bottlenecks.
- **Elastic Stack (ELK)**: A robust solution for logging and analyzing API data.

7. API Documentation Generators Writing API documentation is crucial. Tools like Swagger and Redoc can automatically generate interactive documentation for your APIs based on the code itself.

Chapter 1: Understanding the Fundamentals of APIs

pplication Programming Interfaces (APIs) are the fundamental
building blocks of modern software systems. Whether you're
integrating services, creating mobile applications, or connecting
data sources, understanding how APIs work is crucial. This chapter will
explore the core principles and key elements that make APIs function
efficiently. We will cover HTTP and REST fundamentals, the structure of
API requests and responses, the significance of status codes, and how APIs
compare to web services.

The Basics of HTTP and REST (2000 words)

Understanding HTTP

At the heart of APIs is the Hypertext Transfer Protocol (HTTP), which is
the foundation of communication on the World Wide Web. HTTP allows
browsers, applications, and systems to communicate with servers by sending
requests and receiving responses. An HTTP request follows a client-server
model where a client (browser or application) sends a request to a server, and
the server processes this request and returns a response.

Key Components of HTTP:

- **Client**: The entity making the request (browser, mobile app, backend service).
- **Server**: The entity that receives the request and returns a response.
- **HTTP Methods**: These are specific actions (e.g., GET, POST, PUT, DELETE) that define the intent of the request.
- **Status Codes**: A numeric code that tells the client whether the request was successful or encountered an issue.
- **Headers**: Metadata that provide additional information about the request or response.
- **Body**: The data being sent or received (used in POST, PUT requests).

Understanding REST

Representational State Transfer (REST) is an architectural style designed to exploit the existing protocols of the web, particularly HTTP. RESTful APIs are built to be stateless and rely on a client-server architecture where operations (like CRUD) are performed using HTTP methods.

Key Principles of REST:

1. **Statelessness**: Each request from a client to the server must contain all the information the server needs to fulfill the request. This means no client context is stored on the server between requests.
2. **Client-Server Architecture**: REST separates the concerns of client and server. The server handles the logic, data storage, and communication, while the client interacts with the server to retrieve or manipulate data.
3. **Uniform Interface**: REST relies on a consistent set of rules and conventions that clients follow to communicate with the server. This includes the use of resources (typically represented by URLs) and the use of standard HTTP methods.
4. **Stateless Communication**: Each client request contains all the information the server needs to process the request, independent of previous requests.
5. **Cacheability**: Responses from a REST API should indicate whether or not they are cacheable to improve performance by reducing redundant

network calls.

Example of REST in Action: A simple weather API might expose endpoints such as:

- GET /weather/today: Fetch today's weather data.
- POST /weather: Submit new weather data.
- PUT /weather/today: Update today's weather data.
- DELETE /weather/today: Remove today's weather data from the server.

The simplicity and scalability of REST APIs have made them the most popular method for designing web APIs.

API Requests and Responses: GET, POST, PUT, DELETE (2000 words)

When interacting with an API, the client sends a request to the server, and the server responds based on the data it receives and processes. The structure of this interaction relies on the HTTP methods used in the request. The most common HTTP methods that developers use to interact with APIs are **GET, POST, PUT, and DELETE**. These methods are part of the CRUD operations (Create, Read, Update, Delete) which manage the lifecycle of data.

GET Requests

GET is the method used to retrieve information from a server. When a GET request is made, the server processes the request and returns the requested resource, typically in the form of a JSON or XML response.

- **Use case**: A client requests a list of users, product details, or weather data.
- **Example**: GET /api/v1/products/123 retrieves the product details with the ID 123.
- **Key Characteristics**:
- GET requests are **idempotent**, meaning multiple identical GET requests

13

will yield the same result.

- GET requests do not change the server's state. They are **read-only** operations.

Example: A client wants to retrieve a list of all available books in a library.

```bash
Copy code
GET /api/v1/books
```

This request would return a list of books in JSON format:

```json
Copy code
[
  {
    "id": 1,
    "title": "Introduction to APIs",
    "author": "John Doe"
  },
  {
    "id": 2,
    "title": "Advanced HTTP",
    "author": "Jane Doe"
  }
]
```

POST Requests

POST is used when the client needs to send data to the server to create a new resource. Unlike GET, POST modifies the server's state by submitting new data, such as creating a new user or posting a blog entry.

- **Use case**: Submitting form data, creating new records in a database.
- **Example**: POST /api/v1/products creates a new product.
- **Key Characteristics**:
- POST requests are **not idempotent**, meaning multiple POST requests

will create multiple new resources (i.e., duplicate entries).

- POST requests contain data in the request body, such as a JSON payload.

Example: A client wants to create a new book entry in the library.

```bash
Copy code
POST /api/v1/books
{
    "title": "Understanding APIs",
    "author": "Mark Twain"
}
```

The server would respond with a status indicating success and a reference to the newly created book:

```json
Copy code
{
    "id": 3,
    "title": "Understanding APIs",
    "author": "Mark Twain"
}
```

PUT Requests

PUT is used to update an existing resource or create a new resource if it doesn't already exist. When a PUT request is made, the entire resource is updated with the new data provided by the client.

- **Use case**: Updating user details, modifying an existing blog post.
- **Example**: PUT /api/v1/products/123 updates the product with ID 123.
- **Key Characteristics**:
- PUT is **idempotent**. Making multiple identical PUT requests will yield the same result.
- PUT typically replaces the entire resource with the new representation.

15

Example: A client wants to update the details of an existing book entry.

```bash
Copy code
PUT /api/v1/books/1
{
  "title": "Introduction to API Development",
  "author": "John Doe"
}
```

If the book with ID 1 exists, it will be updated to reflect the new title and author.

DELETE Requests

DELETE is used to remove a resource from the server. When a DELETE request is made, the server deletes the specified resource and returns a confirmation.

- **Use case**: Deleting a user, removing an item from a database.
- **Example**: DELETE /api/v1/products/123 deletes the product with ID 123.
- **Key Characteristics**:
- DELETE is **idempotent**. Deleting the same resource multiple times will result in the same outcome (the resource will no longer exist).
- DELETE operations do not have a body and typically return a status code to indicate success or failure.

Example: A client wants to remove a book from the library.

```bash
Copy code
DELETE /api/v1/books/1
```

The server responds with:

```json
json
Copy code
{
  "message": "Book successfully deleted."
}
```

Status Codes and What They Mean (1500 words)

HTTP status codes are critical in understanding the outcome of a request. They are three-digit numbers returned by the server to indicate the result of the client's request. Understanding these codes is essential for debugging, optimizing, and interacting with APIs.

1xx: Informational Codes

These codes are rarely used in practice but indicate that the server has received the request and is continuing to process it.

- **100 Continue**: The client can continue the request, as everything so far looks fine.
- **101 Switching Protocols**: The server acknowledges a request to switch protocols (e.g., from HTTP to WebSocket).

2xx: Success Codes

These indicate that the request was successfully processed by the server.

- **200 OK**: The request succeeded, and the server has returned the requested data.
- **201 Created**: The request was successful, and a new resource was created (typically returned after a POST request).
- **204 No Content**: The request was successful, but no data is returned (often used with DELETE requests).

Example: After a successful POST request to create a new user, the server

17

responds with:

```json
Copy code
{
  "status": 201,
  "message": "User created successfully"
}
```

3xx: Redirection Codes

These codes indicate that the client must take additional action to complete the request, usually involving being redirected to a different URL.

- **301 Moved Permanently**: The requested resource has been moved to a new URL, and all future requests should be made to this new URL.
- **302 Found**: The resource is temporarily at a different URL, but future requests should continue to be made to the original URL.
- **304 Not Modified**: The resource has not been modified since the last request, and the client can use a cached version of the resource.

4xx: Client Error Codes

These codes indicate that there was an error in the client's request.

- **400 Bad Request**: The request was malformed or invalid.
- **401 Unauthorized**: Authentication is required, and the client has not provided valid credentials.
- **403 Forbidden**: The server understood the request but is refusing to fulfill it.
- **404 Not Found**: The requested resource could not be found on the server.
- **409 Conflict**: The request could not be processed due to a conflict in the request, such as duplicate data.

Example: If a client tries to update a user that does not exist, the server might return:

```json
Copy code
{
  "status": 404,
  "message": "User not found"
}
```

5xx: Server Error Codes

These codes indicate that something went wrong on the server's side.

- **500 Internal Server Error**: The server encountered an unexpected condition that prevented it from fulfilling the request.
- **502 Bad Gateway**: The server received an invalid response from an upstream server.
- **503 Service Unavailable**: The server is currently unable to handle the request due to temporary overload or maintenance.

APIs vs. Web Services (1500 words)

APIs and web services are often mentioned together, but while they are related, they are not the same. Both are used to enable communication between software applications, but there are key differences.

What is a Web Service?

A web service is a standardized way for applications to communicate with each other over a network. Web services are always available over the web and are built on specific protocols (usually SOAP or REST). They expose a collection of operations that are accessible over the web.

There are two main types of web services:

- **SOAP (Simple Object Access Protocol)**: SOAP is a protocol that defines a set of rules for structuring messages to ensure security and reliability. SOAP web services are used in enterprise environments for complex transactions.

- **RESTful Web Services**: These are web services that use HTTP and REST principles to communicate. They are more lightweight and flexible than SOAP services, making them more popular in modern web development.

API vs. Web Service

While all web services are APIs, not all APIs are web services. Here's a breakdown of the key differences:

- **API**: An API is a broad term that refers to any mechanism that allows applications to communicate. It doesn't necessarily have to be over the web; APIs can be local or remote. APIs can be file-based, hardware-based, or web-based.
- **Web Service**: A web service is a specific type of API that is available over the web and uses standard web protocols (HTTP, SOAP, etc.).

Key Differences:

- **Protocol**: Web services typically follow specific protocols (SOAP, REST). APIs, on the other hand, can use any communication protocol.
- **Usage:** APIs can be used for many things beyond web services (e.g., operating system APIs, library APIs), while web services are always internet-based.
- **Performance**: RESTful APIs tend to be more lightweight and faster than SOAP-based web services because they use HTTP and less data overhead.

Example: Comparing API and Web Service

- **Web Service Example (SOAP)**:

```
xml
Copy code
```

```
<soap:Envelope>
    <soap:Body>
        <m:GetTemperature>
            <m:City>New York</m:City>
        </m:GetTemperature>
    </soap:Body>
</soap:Envelope>
```

- **API Example (REST)**:

```
http
Copy code
GET /weather?city=NewYork HTTP/1.1
Host: api.weather.com
```

Both accomplish the same task (fetching weather data), but REST is simpler and easier to work with, especially for web and mobile applications.

When to Use APIs vs. Web Services

- **Use a Web Service (SOAP)**: When you need strict security, reliability, and transaction management (e.g., banking, enterprise systems).
- **Use an API (REST)**: For lightweight, flexible, and scalable web or mobile applications where simplicity and speed are priorities.

Conclusion

In this chapter, we've laid the groundwork for understanding the fundamentals of APIs, exploring key HTTP methods, examining status codes, and drawing distinctions between APIs and web services. Mastering these concepts is critical for building robust, scalable, and reliable APIs. With a firm grasp of HTTP and REST, the next step in API development is learning how to design effective API endpoints, handle authentication, and secure your APIs.

Chapter 2: Designing Your First API

I n this chapter, we'll take you through the essential elements of designing your first API. By the end, you'll have a solid understanding of how to create well-structured, maintainable, and scalable APIs that developers will love. We'll cover the **principles of good API design, API endpoints and URI structuring, the importance of versioning**, and the **best practices for handling query parameters, headers, and payloads**.

Principles of Good API Design (2000 words)

Good API design is crucial because it impacts the usability, scalability, and longevity of your application. APIs are meant to be used by developers, and a well-designed API can significantly enhance developer productivity, ease integration, and reduce maintenance efforts. Let's explore the fundamental principles of good API design:

1. Simplicity and Consistency

The first rule of good API design is **simplicity**. A simple API is easier to understand, adopt, and integrate. Developers should be able to use your API with minimal effort. Keep the API's interface intuitive and predictable, allowing users to learn it quickly without unnecessary complexity.

- **Avoid unnecessary complexity**: Don't overwhelm users with intricate logic or deeply nested routes. Keep things simple by focusing on the core purpose of the API.

- **Consistency**: Use consistent naming conventions, structure, and response formats throughout the API. If your API uses GET /users to retrieve a list of users, it should follow a similar pattern for other resources (e.g., GET /orders for fetching orders).

Consistency also applies to error handling and response codes. For example, all errors should return structured messages that developers can rely on (e.g., JSON format with a clear error code and description).

2. Use RESTful Principles

As we discussed in Chapter 1, REST (Representational State Transfer) is the most widely adopted architectural style for designing APIs. Following REST principles leads to a stateless, scalable, and loosely coupled system.

Key REST principles include:

- **Resource Identification**: Resources (such as users, orders, or products) should be identifiable by URIs (Uniform Resource Identifiers). Each resource should have its unique URI (e.g., /api/users/123 for the user with ID 123).
- **Statelessness**: Every request should carry enough information for the server to understand it without relying on the state of previous requests. This makes the API more scalable and easier to manage.
- **Uniform Interface**: Use standard HTTP methods (GET, POST, PUT, DELETE) consistently to perform operations on resources. Avoid creating custom methods or deviating from the HTTP standard.

3. Use Clear and Meaningful Naming Conventions

Naming is important because it shapes the readability of your API. Resource names should be **nouns**, not verbs, and they should represent the entity being acted upon (e.g., users, products, orders). Avoid including actions in resource names; instead, use HTTP methods to define actions (e.g., GET /users to retrieve users).

- **Plural or Singular**: Use plural nouns for resource collections (/users for a list of users) and singular for specific resources (/users/123 for a single user).
- **Avoid Technical Jargon**: Use terms that are clear to the consumers of your API, avoiding overly technical or domain-specific language unless absolutely necessary.

4. Embrace Hypermedia as the Engine of Application State (HATEOAS)

One of the principles of REST is the use of **HATEOAS** (Hypermedia as the Engine of Application State). This principle means that an API response should include links to related resources or actions that the client can take.

For example, when retrieving a user profile, the response could include links to related resources like the user's posts or friends, allowing the client to navigate through the API without hardcoding URIs.

Here's an example of HATEOAS in action:

```json
Copy code
{
  "id": 123,
  "name": "John Doe",
  "email": "john.doe@example.com",
  "links": {
    "self": "/users/123",
    "posts": "/users/123/posts",
    "friends": "/users/123/friends"
  }
}
```

5. Ensure Flexibility and Scalability

A good API design should be **scalable** and able to handle growth in data volume, traffic, and functionality. Think ahead to how your API might evolve and ensure that your design can accommodate future requirements without needing significant changes.

- **Pagination**: If your API is likely to return large datasets (e.g., lists of users or products), implement pagination. This prevents the API from returning too much data at once, which can overwhelm both the client and server.
- **Filtering and Sorting**: Allow users to filter and sort the data they request. For example, GET /products?category=electronics&sort=price allows users to retrieve only electronic products, sorted by price.

6. Error Handling

Effective error handling is a critical component of good API design. The API should always return informative and standardized error messages that help developers understand what went wrong and how to fix it.

- **Use HTTP Status Codes**: Return the appropriate HTTP status codes for different types of errors (e.g., 404 Not Found, 400 Bad Request, 500 Internal Server Error).
- **Provide Detailed Error Messages**: The response body should include helpful details about the error. For example:

```json
Copy code
{
  "error": {
    "code": 400,
    "message": "Invalid email format",
    "details": "The email field must follow the format:
    user@example.com"
  }
}
```

7. Security and Authentication

Security should be built into the API design from the beginning. Use established authentication and authorization methods like OAuth2, JWT (JSON Web Token), or API keys. Always use HTTPS to encrypt communication between clients and the server.

- **OAuth2**: A secure, token-based authentication system that's widely used by APIs such as Google and Facebook.
- **JWT**: A lightweight and secure method to authenticate users and authorize requests.

8. Versioning

Your API will likely evolve over time as new features are added and old ones are deprecated. Implementing versioning from the start allows you to make changes without breaking existing clients. We will discuss versioning in detail later in this chapter.

API Endpoints and URI Structuring (2000 words)

When designing your API, one of the first things to consider is how to structure the endpoints. The goal is to make the API intuitive and easy to use while adhering to REST principles. A well-designed API should have clearly defined **URI (Uniform Resource Identifier)** patterns that make it easy to identify resources and navigate the API.

1. Resource-Based URIs

At the core of any RESTful API is the concept of resources. Each resource in your system (e.g., users, products, orders) should be represented by a URI. URIs should be clear and descriptive, helping the API consumer understand what resource they're interacting with.

Examples of Resource-Based URIs:

- **Single Resource**: /users/123 refers to the user with ID 123.
- **Resource Collection**: /users refers to the collection of all users.
- **Nested Resources**: If a resource is related to another resource, it's common to nest URIs. For example, /users/123/orders would refer to all orders placed by user 123.

2. Using HTTP Methods Effectively

As discussed in Chapter 1, the combination of HTTP methods (GET, POST, PUT, DELETE) and URIs allows the client to perform different operations on resources. The choice of HTTP method determines the action being performed, while the URI specifies the target resource.

Examples of CRUD Operations:

- **Create a new resource:**
- POST /users creates a new user.
- **Retrieve a resource:**
- GET /users/123 retrieves the user with ID 123.
- **Update a resource:**
- PUT /users/123 updates the user with ID 123.
- **Delete a resource:**
- DELETE /users/123 deletes the user with ID 123.

3. Organizing URIs by Resource Hierarchy

When designing URIs, think about the relationships between resources. Use hierarchical structures to reflect those relationships. For example, if you're building an e-commerce API, an order would be a child resource of a user:

- /users/123/orders/456: Refers to order 456 placed by user 123.

Other examples of hierarchical URIs:

- /companies/789/employees/123: Refers to employee 123 working at company 789.
- /authors/456/books/123: Refers to book 123 written by author 456.

4. Avoiding Verb-Based URIs

A common mistake in API design is embedding actions or verbs in the URI. Instead of using actions like /getUsers or /createUser, use resource-based

URIs and let the HTTP method define the action.

Good URI Examples:

- /users (for listing users or creating a new user with POST)
- /users/123 (for retrieving, updating, or deleting a user)

Bad URI Examples:

- /getUsers
- /createUser
- /deleteUser

The use of HTTP methods should make it clear what action is being performed, so there's no need to include the action in the URI.

5. Handling Relationships Between Resources

In RESTful API design, relationships between resources can be handled in two primary ways:

- **Sub-resources**: Represent relationships between entities through nested URIs. For example, /users/123/orders/456 represents order 456 for user 123. This approach works well when there's a clear parent-child relationship.
- **Linking**: Alternatively, related resources can be represented using HATEOAS (discussed earlier) by providing URLs to related resources in the response body. For example, a GET /users/123 response might include links to the user's orders, friends, and profile.

6. Pagination, Sorting, and Filtering

When designing APIs that deal with large datasets (such as user lists or product catalogs), it's important to implement pagination, sorting, and filtering features. These features allow clients to request only the data they need, reducing the load on the server and improving performance.

- **Pagination**: Use query parameters to paginate large collections. For example, GET /users?page=2&limit=50 retrieves page 2 of users with a limit of 50 users per page.
- **Sorting**: Allow clients to sort the results by specific fields. For example, GET /users?sort=createdAt retrieves users sorted by the createdAt field.
- **Filtering**: Clients may want to filter data based on specific criteria. For example, GET /products?category=electronics&price<1000 retrieves electronic products priced below $1000.

By providing these options, you give API consumers flexibility and reduce the need for them to retrieve and process unnecessary data.

The Importance of Versioning in APIs (1500 words)

Versioning is one of the most important aspects of API design because APIs evolve over time. Without versioning, any changes you make to your API could break existing clients, leading to frustrated users and unreliable services. API versioning ensures backward compatibility, giving developers time to migrate to newer versions without interrupting current workflows.

1. Why API Versioning is Essential

APIs need to change and grow to accommodate new features, fix bugs, or improve performance. However, once an API is in use, these changes can introduce breaking changes for existing clients. Versioning allows API developers to introduce new functionality without disrupting the users who are dependent on the current version.

Common reasons for versioning include:

- **Changing the structure of a resource** (e.g., adding new fields, removing old ones).
- **Introducing new endpoints or modifying existing ones.**
- **Improving performance or changing the underlying architecture.**
- **Fixing security vulnerabilities** or modifying authentication methods.

2. Approaches to API Versioning

There are several ways to implement API versioning, each with its pros and cons.

- **URI Versioning**: The most common approach is to include the version number in the URI. For example:
- /v1/users refers to version 1 of the API.
- /v2/users refers to version 2 of the API.
- This approach is easy to understand and widely adopted but can result in a proliferation of versions and endpoints as the API evolves.
- **Header Versioning**: Instead of embedding the version in the URI, you can pass it as a custom header in the request. For example:

```http
Copy code
GET /users
Accept: application/vnd.myapi.v1+json
```

- This approach keeps the URIs cleaner and focuses on the content type to determine the version, but it's less intuitive for developers to use compared to URI versioning.
- **Query Parameter Versioning**: Another approach is to include the version in the query parameters:
- /users?version=1
- This approach is simple but can clutter the query string and is less commonly used compared to URI versioning.

3. When to Introduce a New Version

A new version should be introduced when changes are made that could break existing clients or change the behavior of the API significantly. Examples include:

- **Changing the response format**: If you modify the structure of a resource (e.g., renaming fields, changing data types), it's important to introduce a new version to avoid breaking clients that depend on the original structure.
- **Adding new functionality**: If the API introduces new features or endpoints, it's often a good idea to version the API to indicate that these are part of a new release.
- **Deprecating old functionality**: When certain endpoints or features are no longer supported, versioning allows you to phase them out without disrupting clients still using them.

4. Best Practices for API Versioning

- **Deprecation Policy**: Clearly communicate when older versions of your API will no longer be supported. Give developers enough time to migrate to the newer version and provide documentation to help with the transition.
- **Backward Compatibility**: Whenever possible, avoid introducing breaking changes. Instead, use versioning to add new features while maintaining backward compatibility with older versions.
- **Documentation**: Keep comprehensive documentation for each version of the API. Ensure that developers can easily find the version they are using and understand how to upgrade to the latest version.

Working with Query Parameters, Headers, and Payloads (1500 words)

APIs often need to accept additional input beyond just the URI. Query parameters, headers, and payloads allow API consumers to provide more information when making requests. Let's explore how each of these elements is used in API design.

1. Query Parameters

Query parameters are key-value pairs appended to the URI after a question mark (?). They are typically used for filtering, sorting, or providing optional parameters.

Examples of Common Query Parameters:

- GET /users?status=active: Retrieves only active users.
- GET /products?category=electronics&sort=price: Filters products by category and sorts by price.
- GET /orders?startDate=2023-01-01&endDate=2023-12-31: Retrieves orders within a specific date range.

Query parameters provide flexibility in how clients request data, allowing them to fine-tune their queries without needing separate endpoints.

2. Headers

Headers are used to pass metadata about the request or response. They are especially useful for providing authentication tokens, specifying content types, or setting preferences like language or compression.

Common Header Fields:

- **Authorization**: Used to pass authentication tokens (e.g., OAuth tokens, JWT tokens).
- Example: Authorization: Bearer <token>
- **Content-Type**: Specifies the format of the request or response body (e.g., JSON, XML).
- Example: Content-Type: application/json
- **Accept**: Informs the server of the content types the client is willing to accept in the response.
- Example: Accept: application/json

Example: An API request with headers for authentication and content type.

```http
Copy code
```

```
GET /api/v1/users
Authorization: Bearer eyJhbGciOiJIUzI1NiIsInR5cCI6IkpXVCJ9...
Accept: application/json
```

Headers are critical for security and interoperability. They enable the client and server to communicate additional information beyond the basic request and response data.

3. Payloads (Body Data)

Payloads are used to send data in POST, PUT, and PATCH requests. While GET and DELETE requests typically don't have a payload, POST and PUT requests require a body to create or update resources.

Examples of Payloads in API Requests:

- **POST /users**: To create a new user, the client sends data in the request body:

```json
Copy code
{
    "name": "John Doe",
    "email": "john.doe@example.com",
    "password": "securepassword"
}
```

- **PUT /users/123**: To update user 123's details, the client sends an updated representation of the user:

```json
Copy code
{
    "name": "John Doe",
```

```
    "email": "john.doe@newdomain.com"
}
```

The structure of the payload is often determined by the **Content-Type** header. For most modern APIs, JSON is the preferred format due to its simplicity and wide support.

4. Best Practices for Handling Query Parameters, Headers, and Payloads

- **Keep query parameters optional**: Use query parameters for optional filters and sorting, not for required data. Required data should be passed in the URI or request body.
- **Validate headers and payloads**: Always validate the input provided by clients in headers and payloads to prevent security vulnerabilities and ensure data integrity.
- **Use appropriate HTTP status codes**: When a request includes invalid query parameters, headers, or payloads, return an appropriate status code (e.g., 400 Bad Request).

Conclusion

In this chapter, we've explored the core principles of designing a well-structured API. From the importance of good design and consistent URIs to the role of versioning and the effective use of query parameters, headers, and payloads, these concepts form the foundation of any robust API. The next step is to delve into more advanced topics, including securing your API, handling authentication, and optimizing performance. As you continue to build out your API, keep these principles in mind to ensure your API is easy to use, scalable, and future-proof.

Chapter 3: RESTful APIs: Best Practices and Patterns

R ESTful APIs have become the standard for building web services due to their simplicity, scalability, and ease of use. This chapter delves into what makes an API RESTful, explores core principles like statelessness and cacheability, provides guidelines for designing scalable and flexible APIs, and presents a case study to illustrate these concepts in action.

What Makes an API RESTful? (2000 words)

Understanding REST

REST (Representational State Transfer) is an architectural style for designing networked applications. It leverages the existing protocols of the web, primarily HTTP, to facilitate communication between clients and servers. RESTful APIs are based on a set of constraints that ensure that they are scalable, reliable, and easy to understand.

Key Characteristics of RESTful APIs

1. **Resource-Based**: In REST, resources (such as users, products, orders) are the primary focus. Each resource is identified by a unique URI (Uniform Resource Identifier). Resources can be represented in various

formats, typically JSON or XML.

2. **Statelessness**: Each client request must contain all the information needed for the server to fulfill that request. This means the server does not store any client context between requests. Statelessness simplifies server design, allowing for easier scaling and recovery.

3. **Cacheability**: Responses from a RESTful API can be marked as cacheable or non-cacheable. This allows clients to cache responses to improve performance and reduce load on the server. Proper cache management is crucial for enhancing the efficiency of the API.

4. **Uniform Interface**: REST APIs adhere to a consistent set of conventions for interacting with resources. This includes using standard HTTP methods (GET, POST, PUT, DELETE) for CRUD operations and a consistent URI structure.

5. **Layered System**: REST allows for a layered architecture, where intermediaries (like proxies and gateways) can be used between clients and servers. This can enhance scalability, security, and performance without the client needing to be aware of these layers.

6. **Code on Demand (Optional)**: REST allows servers to provide executable code (like JavaScript) to clients when necessary. This feature is optional and not widely used but can enhance the functionality of the client.

How REST Differs from Other Architectures

REST is often compared to other architectures like SOAP (Simple Object Access Protocol) and GraphQL:

- **SOAP**: SOAP is a protocol that requires strict adherence to standards and is often more complex to implement. It provides built-in error handling and security features but can be seen as heavyweight compared to REST.
- **GraphQL**: GraphQL allows clients to request only the data they need and offers more flexibility in querying data. However, it can add complexity in terms of query construction and server implementation.

RESTful APIs in the Real World

RESTful APIs are used by many popular web services and applications, including:

- **Twitter**: Provides a RESTful API for posting tweets, retrieving user information, and more.
- **GitHub**: Uses a RESTful API for managing repositories, commits, and issues.
- **Spotify**: Offers a RESTful API for accessing music data, user playlists, and more.

By leveraging the principles of REST, these services offer scalable, efficient, and easy-to-use APIs for developers and users alike.

Statelessness, Cacheability, and Uniform Interface (2000 words)

1. Statelessness

Statelessness is one of the most critical principles of REST architecture. In a stateless system, each request from the client to the server must contain all the information needed to process that request. This includes authentication credentials, parameters, and any contextual information.

Benefits of Statelessness:

- **Scalability**: Since the server does not maintain client state, it can easily handle a large number of requests from multiple clients without needing to track sessions.
- **Reliability**: If a server fails or needs to be replaced, any client can connect to another server to fulfill the request without any loss of context.
- **Simplicity**: Stateless systems are easier to develop, manage, and debug since they don't require complex session management.

Example of Statelessness: When a client requests user data:

```http
http
Copy code
GET /api/v1/users/123 HTTP/1.1
Authorization: Bearer <token>
```

In this example, the request includes the authorization token, allowing the server to authenticate the user without needing to maintain a session.

2. Cacheability

Cacheability is another essential feature of RESTful APIs. Responses from the server should explicitly indicate whether they are cacheable or non-cacheable. This allows clients to cache responses and reuse them for subsequent requests, reducing server load and improving performance.

Benefits of Cacheability:

- **Improved Performance**: By caching responses, clients can reduce the number of requests sent to the server, resulting in faster load times and reduced latency.
- **Reduced Load on Servers**: Caching minimizes the number of requests that need to be processed by the server, allowing it to handle more clients simultaneously.
- **Better User Experience**: Cached responses can provide faster access to data, improving the overall user experience.

How to Implement Cacheability:

- **HTTP Headers**: Use HTTP headers like Cache-Control, Expires, and ETag to manage caching behavior.
- Cache-Control: max-age=3600 indicates that the response can be cached for one hour.
- ETag: "abc123" provides a unique identifier for the resource, allowing clients to check if the cached version is still valid.

Example of Cacheable Response:

```http
http
Copy code
HTTP/1.1 200 OK
Cache-Control: max-age=3600
ETag: "abc123"
Content-Type: application/json

{
  "id": 123,
  "name": "John Doe"
}
```

3. Uniform Interface

The uniform interface is a defining characteristic of RESTful APIs that simplifies and decouples the architecture. It allows different clients to interact with the server in a consistent manner, regardless of the underlying implementation.

Key Constraints of a Uniform Interface:

- **Resource Identification**: Resources should be identifiable through URIs. Each resource has a unique URI that clients use to access it.
- **Standardized Methods**: Use standard HTTP methods (GET, POST, PUT, DELETE) for interacting with resources.
- **Representations**: Clients interact with resources in a consistent manner, receiving representations of the resource (typically JSON or XML).
- **Self-Descriptive Messages**: Each request and response should contain enough information to describe how to process them, including the format and structure.

Benefits of a Uniform Interface:

- **Interoperability**: Clients and servers can be developed independently as long as they adhere to the constraints of the uniform interface.
- **Simplicity**: Reduces the complexity of the API, making it easier for

developers to understand and use.

Example of Uniform Interface: When a client retrieves user data:

```
http
Copy code
GET /api/v1/users/123 HTTP/1.1
Accept: application/json
```

The server responds with a JSON representation of the user:

```
json
Copy code
{
  "id": 123,
  "name": "John Doe",
  "email": "john.doe@example.com"
}
```

How to Design RESTful APIs for Scalability and Flexibility (1500 words)

Designing RESTful APIs for scalability and flexibility is essential for accommodating growth and changes in requirements. Here are best practices for achieving this:

1. Plan Your Resources and Endpoints

Before you start building your API, spend time planning your resources and endpoints. Identify the key resources your API will expose and how they relate to each other. A well-thought-out resource structure makes it easier to scale and extend the API in the future.

- **Resource Mapping**: Create a mapping of your resources and their relationships. For example:
- Users

- Orders
- Products
- **Hierarchical Structure**: Use a hierarchical structure to represent relationships between resources. For example:
- /users/123/orders (orders for user 123)
- /products/456/reviews (reviews for product 456)

2. Implement Versioning from the Start

As mentioned earlier, versioning is crucial for maintaining backward compatibility. By implementing versioning from the start, you can introduce new features and changes without breaking existing clients.

- **URI Versioning**: Include the version number in the URI:
- /api/v1/users
- /api/v2/users
- **Consistent Versioning Strategy**: Develop a clear versioning strategy that defines how you will increment version numbers (e.g., major vs. minor versions).

3. Use Pagination for Large Data Sets

When dealing with large data sets, it's important to implement pagination to prevent overwhelming clients and servers. Pagination allows clients to request a subset of data rather than the entire data set.

Common Pagination Techniques:

- **Offset and Limit**: Specify an offset and limit in the query parameters:
- /api/v1/users?offset=0&limit=10
- **Page-Based**: Use page numbers instead:
- /api/v1/users?page=1&limit=10

4. Implement Filtering and Sorting

Allow clients to filter and sort data to retrieve only the information they need. This reduces the amount of data transferred and improves performance.

Examples of Filtering and Sorting:

- **Filtering**: /api/v1/products?category=electronics
- **Sorting**: /api/v1/products?sort=price

5. Use Caching Strategies

Leverage caching to improve performance and reduce server load. Implement cache strategies based on the resource and its usage patterns.

- **Response Caching**: Use cache headers (like Cache-Control) to control how responses are cached.
- **Client-Side Caching**: Allow clients to cache responses to reduce the number of requests made to the server.

6. Error Handling and Feedback

Implement comprehensive error handling to provide clients with clear feedback. When clients make requests, they should receive meaningful error messages that help them diagnose and fix issues.

Standardized Error Responses:

- Use consistent error codes and structures in your responses:

```json
Copy code
{
  "error": {
    "code": 400,
    "message": "Invalid request parameter",
    "details": "The 'email' field must be a valid email address."
  }
}
```

Case Study: Building a Simple RESTful API (1500 words)

To solidify your understanding of RESTful APIs, let's walk through a case study of building a simple RESTful API for managing a collection of books in a library. This example will illustrate the principles and patterns we've discussed.

Step 1: Define the Resources

The primary resource for our API will be books. Each book will have the following attributes:

- ID
- Title
- Author
- Genre
- Published Date

Step 2: Plan the Endpoints

We'll design the following endpoints to manage our book resource:

- **GET /api/v1/books**: Retrieve a list of all books.
- **GET /api/v1/books/{id}**: Retrieve a specific book by ID.
- **POST /api/v1/books**: Add a new book.
- **PUT /api/v1/books/{id}**: Update an existing book.
- **DELETE /api/v1/books/{id}**: Remove a book.

Step 3: Implement the API

Here's how you could implement the API using Node.js with Express:

Installation:

```bash
Copy code
npm install express body-parser
```

Server Setup:

```javascript
Copy code
const express = require('express');
const bodyParser = require('body-parser');
const app = express();
const port = 3000;

app.use(bodyParser.json());

let books = []; // In-memory storage for books

app.listen(port, () => {
  console.log(`Server running at http://localhost:${port}`);
});
```

Implementing Endpoints:

```javascript
Copy code
// GET /api/v1/books
app.get('/api/v1/books', (req, res) => {
  res.json(books);
});

// GET /api/v1/books/:id
app.get('/api/v1/books/:id', (req, res) => {
  const book = books.find(b => b.id === parseInt(req.params.id));
  if (!book) return res.status(404).send('Book not found');
  res.json(book);
});

// POST /api/v1/books
app.post('/api/v1/books', (req, res) => {
  const { title, author, genre, publishedDate } = req.body;
  const book = {
    id: books.length + 1,
    title,
```

```
    author,
    genre,
    publishedDate
  };
  books.push(book);
  res.status(201).json(book);
});

// PUT /api/v1/books/:id
app.put('/api/v1/books/:id', (req, res) => {
  const book = books.find(b => b.id === parseInt(req.params.id));
  if (!book) return res.status(404).send('Book not found');

  const { title, author, genre, publishedDate } = req.body;
  book.title = title;
  book.author = author;
  book.genre = genre;
  book.publishedDate = publishedDate;

  res.json(book);
});

// DELETE /api/v1/books/:id
app.delete('/api/v1/books/:id', (req, res) => {
  const bookIndex = books.findIndex(b => b.id ===
  parseInt(req.params.id));
  if (bookIndex === -1) return res.status(404).send('Book not
  found');

  books.splice(bookIndex, 1);
  res.status(204).send();
});
```

Step 4: Testing the API

After implementing the API, it's essential to test its functionality. Use tools like Postman to make requests to the endpoints and validate the expected responses.

1. **Retrieve All Books:**

- **Request**: GET /api/v1/books
- **Response**: [] (empty array)

1. **Add a New Book**:

- **Request**:

```json
Copy code
POST /api/v1/books
{
   "title": "The Great Gatsby",
   "author": "F. Scott Fitzgerald",
   "genre": "Fiction",
   "publishedDate": "1925-04-10"
}
```

- **Response**: 201 Created with the book details.

1. **Retrieve a Specific Book**:

- **Request**: GET /api/v1/books/1
- **Response**: The details of the book added earlier.

1. **Update a Book**:

- **Request**:

```json
Copy code
PUT /api/v1/books/1
{
```

```
  "title": "The Great Gatsby",
  "author": "F. Scott Fitzgerald",
  "genre": "Classic Fiction",
  "publishedDate": "1925-04-10"
}
```

- **Response**: Updated book details.

1. **Delete a Book**:

- **Request**: DELETE /api/v1/books/1
- **Response**: 204 No Content

Conclusion

In this chapter, we explored the principles that make an API RESTful, including statelessness, cacheability, and uniform interfaces. We discussed best practices for designing scalable and flexible RESTful APIs and walked through a case study to illustrate these concepts in action. By following these principles and patterns, you can create APIs that are easy to use, maintain, and scale as your application grows. The next chapter will focus on securing your RESTful APIs, ensuring they are robust against threats and vulnerabilities.

Chapter 4: Authentication and Authorization in APIs

I n the age of digital transformation, securing APIs has become a critical concern for developers and organizations alike. APIs are often gateways to sensitive data and functionalities, making them attractive targets for malicious actors. This chapter will delve into the crucial aspects of API security, focusing on authentication and authorization processes. We will cover foundational security concepts, practical implementation methods, and advanced techniques to ensure robust security in your APIs.

Introduction to API Security Concepts (2000 words)

Understanding API Security

API security refers to the practice of protecting APIs from unauthorized access and ensuring that only legitimate users can access and manipulate data. This encompasses various techniques and protocols designed to safeguard sensitive information while allowing legitimate users to perform their intended operations.

The Importance of API Security

1. **Data Protection**: APIs often expose sensitive data, including user information, payment details, and proprietary business logic. Protecting

this data is crucial to prevent data breaches, identity theft, and financial fraud.

2. **Preventing Unauthorized Access**: Without proper security measures, APIs can be exploited by attackers who attempt to gain unauthorized access to systems and data. This can lead to data manipulation, service disruption, or even total system compromise.

3. **Compliance and Regulations**: Many industries are governed by strict regulations (e.g., GDPR, HIPAA) that mandate the protection of sensitive information. Implementing strong API security measures is often necessary to achieve compliance and avoid legal repercussions.

4. **Maintaining Trust**: Users trust organizations to handle their data responsibly. Security breaches can severely damage an organization's reputation and erode customer trust.

5. **Securing Business Logic**: APIs often implement business logic that, if compromised, could lead to significant financial losses. Securing the API ensures that business rules and processes remain intact.

Key Security Concepts in APIs

To effectively secure APIs, it is essential to understand several key concepts:

- **Authentication**: This is the process of verifying the identity of a user or system. It ensures that the entity accessing the API is who they claim to be.
- **Authorization**: Once an entity is authenticated, authorization determines what that entity is allowed to do. This involves defining roles and permissions for users or applications.
- **Encryption**: Data encryption protects data in transit and at rest. It ensures that sensitive information is unreadable to unauthorized parties.
- **Tokenization**: This refers to the process of replacing sensitive data with unique identification symbols (tokens) that retain essential information without compromising security.
- **Rate Limiting**: This technique limits the number of requests a client can make to an API within a specific timeframe, helping prevent abuse

and denial-of-service attacks.

- **CORS (Cross-Origin Resource Sharing)**: CORS is a security feature that restricts how resources on a web page can be requested from another domain. Properly configuring CORS settings is crucial for securing APIs.

Implementing Basic Auth and API Keys (2000 words)

1. Basic Authentication

Basic Authentication is one of the simplest methods of securing APIs. It involves sending a username and password with each request, typically encoded in Base64 format. This approach is easy to implement but has limitations regarding security.

How Basic Authentication Works:

1. The client sends an HTTP request to the server without authentication credentials.
2. The server responds with a 401 Unauthorized status code and a WWW-Authenticate header indicating that Basic Authentication is required.
3. The client prompts the user for credentials (username and password).
4. The client sends the credentials in the following format:

```http
Copy code
Authorization: Basic <base64-encoded-credentials>
```

1. Example:

```http
Copy code
```

Authorization: Basic dXNlcm5hbWU6cGFzc3dvcmQ=

1. The server decodes the credentials, verifies them, and, if valid, grants access to the requested resource.

Limitations of Basic Authentication:

- **Security Risks**: Basic Auth transmits credentials in Base64 encoding, which is easily reversible. If the API is not accessed over HTTPS, credentials can be intercepted by attackers.
- **Credential Exposure**: Every request includes the username and password, increasing the risk of exposure if the credentials are compromised.
- **No Session Management**: Basic Authentication does not maintain session state, requiring repeated transmission of credentials for every request.

Best Practices for Using Basic Authentication:

- Always use HTTPS to encrypt the data in transit.
- Limit the use of Basic Authentication to internal APIs or environments where security can be controlled.
- Consider using it in conjunction with other security measures like IP whitelisting or rate limiting.

2. API Keys

API keys are a more common method for authenticating requests to APIs. An API key is a unique identifier assigned to a user or application that is included in API requests. This allows the server to identify and authenticate the client without requiring a username and password.

How API Keys Work:

1. The client registers for an API key with the service provider.

2. The service provider generates a unique key and provides it to the client.
3. The client includes the API key in their requests, either as a query parameter or as a request header.

- As a query parameter:

```http
Copy code
GET /api/v1/users?api_key=your_api_key
```

- As a request header:

```http
Copy code
Authorization: ApiKey your_api_key
```

Benefits of Using API Keys:

- **Simplicity**: API keys are straightforward to implement and require minimal configuration.
- **Statelessness**: Unlike Basic Auth, API keys do not require users to send credentials repeatedly.
- **Rate Limiting**: API keys can be used to enforce rate limits and track usage per user or application.

Limitations of API Keys:

- **Lack of Granularity**: API keys do not provide fine-grained access control. All users with the same key have the same level of access.
- **Potential Exposure**: If an API key is exposed (e.g., in client-side code),

it can be used by unauthorized parties to access the API.

Best Practices for API Key Management:

- Generate unique keys for each user or application and store them securely.
- Implement a system for rotating API keys regularly.
- Monitor usage patterns to identify suspicious activity or abuse.
- Allow users to revoke their API keys as needed.

OAuth2 and JWT Explained (2000 words)

1. Introduction to OAuth2

OAuth2 is an open standard for access delegation commonly used for token-based authentication. It allows third-party applications to access user data without sharing credentials. OAuth2 provides a secure and flexible framework for authorizing access to APIs.

Key Components of OAuth2:

- **Resource Owner**: The user who owns the data and grants access to it.
- **Client**: The application that wants to access the user's data.
- **Authorization Server**: The server that authenticates the resource owner and issues access tokens.
- **Resource Server**: The server that hosts the protected resources (APIs).

2. OAuth2 Flow

OAuth2 defines several authorization flows, but the **Authorization Code Grant** is the most common for web applications.

Authorization Code Grant Flow:

1. The client redirects the user to the authorization server's authorization endpoint, requesting access to specific resources.
2. The resource owner (user) logs in and grants permission to the client.

3. The authorization server redirects the user back to the client with an authorization code.

4. The client exchanges the authorization code for an access token by making a request to the authorization server's token endpoint.

5. The client uses the access token to make requests to the resource server on behalf of the user.

Diagram of the OAuth2 Flow:

```arduino
Copy code
User → Authorization Server (Authorize) → Client↓

Client → Authorization Server (Access Token Request)↓

Authorization Server → Client (Access Token)↓

Client → Resource Server (Access Protected Resource)
```

3. JSON Web Tokens (JWT)

JWT is a compact, URL-safe means of representing claims to be transferred between two parties. It is commonly used in conjunction with OAuth2 for token-based authentication.

Structure of a JWT: A JWT is composed of three parts:

1. **Header:** Contains metadata about the token, such as the signing algorithm used.

```json
Copy code
{
  "alg": "HS256",
  "typ": "JWT"
}
```

1. **Payload**: Contains the claims (statements about an entity). Claims can be standard (like iss, exp, sub) or custom.

```json
Copy code
{
  "sub": "1234567890",
  "name": "John Doe",
  "admin": true
}
```

1. **Signature**: The header and payload are encoded and then signed with a secret or a public/private key pair. This ensures the token's integrity and authenticity.

Example of a JWT:

```plaintext
Copy code
eyJhbGciOiJIUzI1NiIsInR5cCI6IkpXVCJ9.
eyJzdWIiOiIxMjM0NTY3ODkwIiwibmFtZSI6I
kpvaG4gRG9lIiwibWFya0JpbGxpb24iOnRydWV9.
eyJzdWIiOiIxMjM0NTY3ODkwIiwibmF
tZSI6IkpvaG4gRG9lIiwib
WFya0JpbGxpb24iOnRydWV9
```

4. Advantages of JWT

- **Compact**: JWTs are small in size and can be easily transmitted via URLs, POST parameters, or HTTP headers.
- **Self-contained**: JWTs contain all the information needed for authentication, reducing the need to query a database for every request.
- **Stateless**: Since JWTs can be verified without server-side storage,

they work well in stateless environments, making them suitable for microservices architectures.

5. Implementing OAuth2 with JWT in APIs

To secure an API using OAuth2 and JWT, follow these steps:

1. **User Authentication**: Implement the OAuth2 authorization flow to allow users to authenticate with their credentials.
2. **Token Generation**: Once authenticated, generate a JWT for the user, including claims such as user ID and roles.
3. **Token Storage**: Send the JWT to the client, who will store it (usually in local storage or a secure cookie).
4. **Using the Token**: When the client makes requests to the API, include the JWT in the Authorization header:

```http
Copy code
Authorization: Bearer <your_jwt_token>
```

1. **Token Verification**: On the server side, verify the JWT on every request. If valid, allow access to the protected resource.

Securing API Endpoints Based on User Roles (1500 words)

1. Role-Based Access Control (RBAC)

Role-Based Access Control (RBAC) is a method of regulating access to resources based on the roles assigned to individual users. This approach simplifies the management of permissions and enhances security by limiting access to sensitive operations.

2. Implementing RBAC in APIs

When designing an API, consider implementing RBAC to control access to various endpoints. Here's how to do it effectively:

1. **Define Roles**: Identify the different roles in your application and the permissions associated with each role. Common roles include:

- **Admin**: Full access to all resources and administrative functions.
- **User**: Limited access to personal data and basic functionalities.
- **Guest**: Minimal access, often read-only for public resources.

1. **Assign Roles to Users**: When a user is created, assign them one or more roles based on their function in the system. This can be done during user registration or by an administrator.
2. **Protect API Endpoints**: Implement middleware in your API to check user roles against the required permissions for each endpoint.

Example of Protecting Endpoints with RBAC:

```javascript
Copy code
// Middleware for role checking
function checkRole(role) {
  return function(req, res, next) {
    const userRole = req.user.role; // Assume user role is
    attached to req
    if (userRole === role) {
      return next();
    }
    return res.status(403).json({ message: 'Access denied' });
  };
}

// Protecting an endpoint
app.delete('/api/v1/users/:id', checkRole('Admin'), (req, res) => {
  // Logic for deleting a user
});
```

3. Claims-Based Authorization

Another approach to authorization is claims-based authorization, where the access decision is based on the claims included in the JWT. This method allows for a more granular level of access control.

1. **Claims in JWT**: Include user roles and permissions as claims in the JWT. For example:

```json
Copy code
{
  "sub": "1234567890",
  "name": "John Doe",
  "roles": ["admin", "user"]
}
```

1. **Authorize Based on Claims**: When verifying the JWT, check the claims to determine if the user has the necessary permissions to access a specific resource.

Example of Claims-Based Authorization:

```javascript
Copy code
// Middleware for claims checking
function checkPermissions(permission) {
  return function(req, res, next) {
    const userClaims = req.user.claims; // Assume claims are
    attached to req
    if (userClaims.includes(permission)) {
      return next();
    }
    return res.status(403).json({ message: 'Access denied' });
  };
}
```

```
// Protecting an endpoint
app.post('/api/v1/products', checkPermissions('create:product'),
(req, res) => {
  // Logic for creating a product
});
```

4. Testing and Monitoring API Security

Once you have implemented authentication and authorization mechanisms, it's essential to test and monitor the security of your API continuously.

- **Testing**: Perform regular penetration testing and vulnerability assessments to identify weaknesses in your API. Tools like OWASP ZAP or Burp Suite can help automate this process.
- **Monitoring**: Use logging and monitoring solutions to track API usage, identify suspicious activity, and respond to potential security incidents. Tools like ELK Stack (Elasticsearch, Logstash, Kibana) or Splunk can provide insights into API traffic patterns and anomalies.

Conclusion

In this chapter, we explored the crucial concepts of authentication and authorization in APIs. Understanding API security is vital for protecting sensitive data and ensuring that only authorized users can access your services. We covered basic authentication methods, the OAuth2 framework with JWT, and role-based access control strategies. As you move forward, remember that securing APIs is an ongoing process that requires vigilance, testing, and adaptation to new threats. The next chapter will delve into additional API security measures, including data encryption, rate limiting, and securing data in transit.

Chapter 5: API Documentation: The Key to Developer Adoption

I n today's digital landscape, application programming interfaces (APIs) are the backbone of software integration, enabling disparate systems to communicate seamlessly. However, for developers to leverage the power of an API effectively, comprehensive and well-structured documentation is crucial. API documentation serves as a roadmap, guiding developers through the capabilities of an API, outlining how to integrate it into their applications, and ultimately driving adoption.

This chapter will delve into the importance of API documentation, introduce tools for generating documentation, offer best practices for writing clear and concise API docs, and provide strategies to enhance the developer experience. By the end of this chapter, you will have a solid understanding of how to create effective API documentation that facilitates developer adoption and engagement.

Why API Documentation Matters

1. Facilitating Integration

Effective API documentation is essential for helping developers understand how to integrate with an API successfully. It provides the necessary information on endpoints, request formats, response structures, and authentication mechanisms. Clear documentation eliminates ambiguity and confusion, allowing developers to implement integrations with confidence.

- **Example**: Consider an e-commerce platform providing a payment processing API. Comprehensive documentation outlining the necessary endpoints, required parameters, and sample requests will empower developers to integrate the API into their checkout processes seamlessly.

2. Reducing Development Time

Well-documented APIs save developers time by providing quick access to the information they need. When developers can easily find answers to their questions, they spend less time troubleshooting and more time building. This efficiency leads to faster development cycles and improved productivity.

- **Example**: If a developer encounters an issue while integrating with an API, they can quickly reference the documentation to identify the correct parameters or troubleshoot errors, reducing the need for back-and-forth communication with the API provider.

3. Enhancing Developer Experience

API documentation is not just a technical requirement; it also plays a crucial role in shaping the overall developer experience. Well-structured documentation enhances usability and encourages developers to engage with the API.

- **Example**: APIs with comprehensive documentation, clear examples, and user-friendly formatting create a positive experience for developers. In contrast, poorly documented APIs may lead to frustration and ultimately deter developers from using the service.

4. Supporting Developer Onboarding

For organizations that provide APIs, documentation is a critical component of the onboarding process for new developers. Clear and concise documentation helps new users quickly understand the API's functionality and how to use it effectively.

- **Example**: A developer joining a team that uses an API can refer to the documentation to learn about its capabilities, endpoints, and best practices. This onboarding process ensures that new developers can contribute to projects more quickly.

5. Driving API Adoption and Community Growth

High-quality API documentation can foster a thriving developer community around the API. When developers find it easy to understand and use an API, they are more likely to adopt it, share their experiences, and contribute to its growth.

- **Example**: APIs with robust documentation often attract a larger user base, leading to increased visibility and engagement within the developer community. This community can provide valuable feedback and contribute to the API's improvement over time.

Tools for Generating API Documentation

1. Swagger (OpenAPI)

Swagger, now known as OpenAPI, is one of the most widely used tools for designing, documenting, and testing APIs. It provides a standard specification for describing APIs, making it easier for developers to understand their functionality.

Key Features of Swagger:

- **Interactive Documentation**: Swagger UI generates interactive documentation that allows developers to explore and test API endpoints directly from the browser.
- **Code Generation**: Swagger can generate client libraries, server stubs, and API documentation in various programming languages, streamlining the development process.
- **Standardization**: The OpenAPI specification provides a standardized format for documenting APIs, making it easier for developers to understand the API structure and capabilities.

Getting Started with Swagger:

1. **Define Your API**: Use the OpenAPI Specification to define your API endpoints, request parameters, and response structures in a YAML or JSON format.
2. **Generate Documentation**: Use Swagger UI to generate interactive documentation that developers can easily explore and test.
3. **Integrate into Your Workflow**: Incorporate Swagger into your API development workflow to ensure that documentation remains up-to-date as the API evolves.

2. Postman

Postman is a popular tool for testing APIs and provides features for generating documentation based on your API collections. It allows developers to create, organize, and share API requests, making it easier to collaborate and document APIs.

Key Features of Postman:

- **API Collections**: Postman allows you to group related API requests into collections, providing a clear structure for documentation.
- **Automatic Documentation Generation**: Postman can automatically generate documentation based on your API requests and responses, saving time and effort.
- **Collaborative Workspaces**: Postman provides collaborative features, allowing teams to share collections and documentation, making it easier to keep everyone aligned.

Getting Started with Postman:

1. **Create a Collection**: Organize your API requests into collections, grouping related endpoints for clarity.
2. **Document Requests**: Add descriptions, parameters, and example responses to each request within the collection.
3. **Generate Documentation**: Use Postman's documentation feature to generate a shareable, user-friendly format that developers can access easily.

3. Redoc

Redoc is another powerful tool for generating API documentation from OpenAPI specifications. It provides a clean, responsive layout that enhances the user experience.

Key Features of Redoc:

- **Interactive and Responsive UI**: Redoc offers an interactive documentation experience that adapts to different screen sizes, ensuring usability across devices.
- **Support for Markdown**: Redoc supports Markdown, allowing you to enrich your documentation with formatting, links, and images.
- **Customizable**: Redoc provides options for customization, enabling you to tailor the documentation appearance to align with your branding.

Getting Started with Redoc:

1. **Create OpenAPI Specification**: Define your API using the OpenAPI Specification in YAML or JSON format.
2. **Integrate Redoc**: Include Redoc in your project to serve the documentation, or host it separately for public access.
3. **Customize as Needed**: Adjust the appearance and layout to fit your branding and user experience goals.

Writing Clear and Concise API Docs (2000 words)

Writing effective API documentation requires clarity, conciseness, and a user-centered approach. Here are key practices for creating clear and concise API docs:

1. Use a Structured Format

A well-structured format enhances readability and usability. Organize your documentation into clearly defined sections:

- **Overview**: Provide a high-level overview of the API, its purpose, and key features.
- **Authentication**: Explain authentication methods required to access the API.
- **Endpoints**: Document each endpoint with detailed information on

methods, parameters, request and response examples, and error codes.

- **Rate Limiting and Usage Guidelines**: Include any restrictions on API usage and best practices for developers.

2. Write Clear Descriptions

Clarity is essential for effective communication. Use simple, straightforward language to describe your API and its functionality.

- **Avoid Jargon**: Minimize the use of technical jargon or acronyms without explanation. Aim for language that is accessible to developers of all experience levels.
- **Be Specific**: Clearly outline the purpose of each endpoint, its parameters, and the expected results. Use examples to illustrate how to use the API effectively.

3. Include Code Examples

Code examples are invaluable for demonstrating how to use your API. They help developers understand the practical application of the API.

- **Provide Multiple Examples**: Include examples in various programming languages to cater to a broader audience. Offer sample requests and responses for each endpoint.
- **Use Realistic Scenarios**: Present examples that reflect real-world use cases, making it easier for developers to relate to and implement.

4. Document Error Responses

Documenting error responses is essential for helping developers troubleshoot issues effectively.

- **Error Codes and Messages**: Clearly outline the error codes and their meanings, along with examples of error messages. Provide guidance on how to resolve common errors.

- **HTTP Status Codes**: Include HTTP status codes to indicate the success or failure of requests. Document the significance of each status code related to the API.

5. Keep It Up-to-Date

API documentation should evolve alongside the API itself. Ensure that your documentation remains accurate and relevant by regularly updating it.

- **Version Control**: Implement versioning for your API documentation. Clearly indicate changes, deprecated endpoints, and new features in each version.
- **Feedback Loop**: Encourage users to provide feedback on documentation. Use this feedback to identify areas for improvement and enhance clarity.

6. Enhance Usability with Search and Navigation

User-friendly navigation and search features can significantly improve the usability of your API documentation.

- **Table of Contents**: Include a table of contents to help users quickly find the information they need.
- **Search Functionality**: Implement a search feature that allows users to find specific endpoints, terms, or topics within the documentation.

Chapter 6: Error Handling and Response Codes

I n the world of API development, robust error handling and the proper use of response codes are critical components of a well-designed API. Users and developers rely on clear communication about the status of their requests and how to address any issues that arise. In this chapter, we will explore the best practices for error handling, delve into the different types of response codes, and provide guidelines for creating informative error responses. By the end of this chapter, you will have a solid understanding of how to enhance the reliability and usability of your APIs through effective error management.

Introduction to Error Handling in APIs (1000 words)

Importance of Error Handling

Error handling is an essential aspect of API design that ensures users receive meaningful feedback when things go wrong. Proper error management leads to better user experience, improved application reliability, and easier debugging for developers. In a well-designed API, errors should be handled gracefully, providing users with clear information on what went wrong and how they can address the issue.

1. **User Experience**: Users interacting with your API expect to receive clear and actionable feedback when errors occur. Ambiguous or uninformative error messages can lead to frustration and abandonment of your API.

2. **Debugging and Troubleshooting**: For developers using your API, detailed error messages and response codes can significantly simplify the process of diagnosing and fixing issues. Providing context around the error helps users understand what went wrong and how to resolve it.

3. **Service Reliability**: Well-implemented error handling can prevent minor issues from escalating into significant service outages. By managing errors effectively, you can maintain the overall stability of your API.

4. **Security**: Proper error handling can help prevent information leakage about your API's implementation, which could be exploited by malicious users. Careful design of error responses ensures that sensitive data is not exposed.

Common Types of Errors in APIs

Errors can arise from various sources, and understanding the types of errors your API may encounter is crucial for effective error handling. Here are some common categories of errors:

- **Client Errors**: These errors occur when the client sends an invalid request. Examples include:
- Invalid parameters (e.g., missing required fields).
- Unsupported media types.
- Incorrect authentication credentials.
- **Server Errors**: These errors occur on the server side and indicate that something has gone wrong while processing the request. Examples include:
- Internal server errors (500 status).
- Service unavailable (503 status).

- **Network Errors**: Issues related to network connectivity can also lead to errors, including timeouts and unreachable services.
- **Data Errors**: These errors occur when the data provided by the client does not meet the server's requirements or when the server encounters issues while processing the data.

Best Practices for Error Handling (2000 words)

1. Consistent Error Responses
One of the most important aspects of effective error handling is providing consistent error responses. This consistency allows developers to parse and handle errors uniformly, regardless of the specific error encountered.

- **Standard Structure**: Define a standard structure for your error responses. A common format includes the following fields:
- **Status Code**: The HTTP status code indicating the error type.
- **Error Code**: A unique code representing the specific error (for easier categorization).
- **Message**: A human-readable description of the error.
- **Details**: Optional field for additional context, such as validation errors.

Example of a Consistent Error Response:

```json
Copy code
{
  "status": 400,
  "errorCode": "INVALID_REQUEST",
  "message": "The request is missing required parameters.",
  "details": {
    "missingFields": ["email", "password"]
  }
}
```

2. Use Appropriate HTTP Status Codes

HTTP status codes play a vital role in conveying the result of an API request. Using the correct status codes helps clients understand the nature of the error and take appropriate actions.

Common HTTP Status Codes for Error Handling:

- **400 Bad Request**: Indicates that the server could not understand the request due to invalid syntax or missing parameters.
- **401 Unauthorized**: Indicates that the request requires user authentication or the provided credentials are invalid.
- **403 Forbidden**: Indicates that the server understood the request but refuses to authorize it.
- **404 Not Found**: Indicates that the requested resource could not be found on the server.
- **500 Internal Server Error**: Indicates that the server encountered an unexpected condition that prevented it from fulfilling the request.
- **503 Service Unavailable**: Indicates that the server is currently unable to handle the request due to temporary overload or maintenance.

3. Categorizing Errors

Categorizing errors can help clients better understand the types of issues they may encounter. Consider defining categories for your errors based on their nature. For example:

- **Validation Errors**: Errors related to input validation.
- **Authentication Errors**: Errors related to user authentication.
- **Authorization Errors**: Errors related to permission issues.
- **Not Found Errors**: Errors indicating that the requested resource does not exist.
- **Server Errors**: Errors indicating issues on the server side.

Using these categories can simplify error handling for clients, allowing them to implement specific logic based on error types.

4. Detailed Error Messages

Providing detailed error messages can significantly enhance the user experience. When an error occurs, consider including relevant information that can help developers diagnose the issue.

- **Contextual Information**: Provide additional context that helps explain why the error occurred. This could include information about the specific field causing the validation error or hints on how to fix it.

Example of a Detailed Error Message:

```json
Copy code
{
  "status": 422,
  "errorCode": "VALIDATION_ERROR",
  "message": "Validation failed for the provided data.",
  "details": {
    "email": {
      "message": "Email format is invalid.",
      "example": "user@example.com"
    },
    "password": {
      "message": "Password must be at least 8 characters long."
    }
  }
}
```

5. Logging Errors

Logging errors is crucial for maintaining an effective API. Comprehensive logging helps developers understand the frequency and nature of errors and can assist in identifying and fixing issues promptly.

- **Structured Logging**: Use structured logging formats (like JSON) to ensure logs are easy to parse and analyze. Include relevant metadata such as timestamps, request IDs, and user information to help with troubleshooting.

- **Monitoring Tools**: Use monitoring tools (like ELK Stack, Splunk, or Sentry) to aggregate and analyze logs in real time. These tools can provide insights into error patterns and help track the health of your API.

6. Providing Documentation for Errors

Documenting the error codes and their meanings can be invaluable for API users. Create a dedicated section in your API documentation that outlines all possible errors, their status codes, and descriptions.

- **Clear Descriptions**: Ensure that each error code has a clear description that helps users understand the circumstances under which it occurs.
- **Example Responses**: Include example error responses for each code in your documentation. This allows developers to see how to handle errors effectively.

HTTP Response Codes Overview (1500 words)

Understanding HTTP Response Codes

HTTP response codes are standardized codes issued by the server in response to client requests. These codes provide information about the outcome of the request and are categorized into five classes:

1. **1xx Informational**: Indicates that the request was received and is being processed. These codes are rarely used in APIs.
2. **2xx Success**: Indicates that the request was successfully processed. Common codes include:

- **200 OK**: The request succeeded.
- **201 Created**: A new resource was successfully created (usually in response to POST requests).
- **204 No Content**: The request succeeded, but there is no content to return.

1. **3xx Redirection**: Indicates that further action is needed to complete the request. Common codes include:

- **301 Moved Permanently**: The resource has moved to a new URL.
- **302 Found**: The resource is temporarily located at a different URL.

1. **4xx Client Errors**: Indicates that the request contained errors or could not be processed. Common codes include:

- **400 Bad Request**: The server could not understand the request due to malformed syntax.
- **401 Unauthorized**: The request requires user authentication.
- **403 Forbidden**: The server understood the request but refuses to authorize it.
- **404 Not Found**: The server cannot find the requested resource.

1. **5xx Server Errors**: Indicates that the server failed to fulfill a valid request. Common codes include:

- **500 Internal Server Error**: The server encountered an unexpected condition.
- **502 Bad Gateway**: The server received an invalid response from the upstream server.
- **503 Service Unavailable**: The server is currently unable to handle the request due to overload or maintenance.

Best Practices for Using HTTP Response Codes

- **Use the Correct Status Code**: Always use the appropriate status code for the outcome of the request. This helps clients understand the result without needing to parse the response body.
- **Provide Detailed Error Information**: Alongside the status code, include detailed error messages to guide users in resolving the issue.

- **Avoid Overuse of 200 OK**: Be cautious about using the 200 OK status for every successful operation. For example, when creating a resource, use 201 Created instead.

Creating Informative Error Responses (2000 words)

1. Standardizing Error Response Format

To provide a consistent experience for users of your API, define a standardized format for error responses. This structure should include essential fields such as:

- **Status Code**: The HTTP status code associated with the error.
- **Error Code**: A unique identifier for the error (if applicable).
- **Message**: A human-readable description of the error.
- **Details**: Additional context or information related to the error.

Example of a Standardized Error Response:

```json
Copy code
{
   "status": 404,
   "errorCode": "NOT_FOUND",
   "message": "The requested resource was not found.",
   "details": {
      "resource": "User",
      "id": "123"
   }
}
```

2. Error Handling Middleware

Implementing error handling middleware can centralize error management in your API, ensuring that all errors are processed consistently. This approach allows you to define a single location for handling errors, improving maintainability and reducing duplication.

Example of Error Handling Middleware in Express (Node.js):

```javascript
Copy code
function errorHandler(err, req, res, next) {
  console.error(err); // Log the error

  const response = {
    status: err.status || 500,
    errorCode: err.code || "INTERNAL_SERVER_ERROR",
    message: err.message || "An unexpected error occurred.",
    details: err.details || {},
  };

  res.status(response.status).json(response);
}

// Use the middleware
app.use(errorHandler);
```

3. Handling Validation Errors

Validation errors occur when the client submits invalid data. Providing detailed feedback about validation errors is crucial for improving the user experience. Ensure that your API responds with specific information about which fields are invalid and why.

Example of Validation Error Response:

```json
Copy code
{
  "status": 422,
  "errorCode": "VALIDATION_ERROR",
  "message": "Validation failed for one or more fields.",
  "details": {
    "username": {
      "message": "Username is required.",
      "code": "MISSING_FIELD"
```

```
  },
  "email": {
    "message": "Email format is invalid.",
    "code": "INVALID_FORMAT"
  }
 }
}
```

4. Error Handling for Authentication and Authorization

When handling authentication and authorization errors, provide clear feedback to the client about what went wrong. This includes indicating whether the credentials were missing, invalid, or if the user lacks the necessary permissions.

Example of Authentication Error Response:

```json
Copy code
{
  "status": 401,
  "errorCode": "UNAUTHORIZED",
  "message": "Authentication credentials are missing or invalid."
}
```

Example of Authorization Error Response:

```json
Copy code
{
  "status": 403,
  "errorCode": "FORBIDDEN",
  "message": "You do not have permission to access this resource."
}
```

Conclusion

In this chapter, we explored the critical aspects of error handling and response codes in API development. Proper error management not only enhances user experience but also facilitates easier debugging and maintenance. We covered best practices for consistent error responses, the importance of using appropriate HTTP status codes, and strategies for handling specific error types effectively.

As you design and develop your APIs, remember that robust error handling is an essential part of creating a reliable and user-friendly service. The next chapter will delve into additional aspects of API design, including documentation best practices, which are vital for helping users understand and integrate with your API successfully.

Chapter 7: Testing APIs: Ensuring Reliability and Performance

Chapter 7: Testing APIs: Ensuring Reliability and Performance

APIs serve as the backbone of modern applications, facilitating communication between different systems and enabling seamless integration. As the reliance on APIs continues to grow, ensuring their reliability and performance has become paramount. Rigorous testing is essential to confirm that APIs behave as expected, handle various scenarios, and provide consistent performance. In this chapter, we will explore the essential aspects of API testing, including unit testing of API endpoints, various tools for testing APIs, writing integration tests, and automating API testing within CI/CD pipelines.

Unit Testing Your API Endpoints

1. What is Unit Testing?

Unit testing is a fundamental testing methodology that focuses on verifying the smallest parts of an application—typically individual functions or methods— to ensure they work correctly. For APIs, this means testing specific endpoints to confirm that they produce the expected results given certain inputs.

Key Benefits of Unit Testing:

Early Detection of Bugs: Unit tests help identify issues at an early stage, reducing the cost and time associated with fixing bugs later in the development cycle.

Documentation: Well-written unit tests serve as documentation for your API, illustrating how the endpoints are intended to be used.

Facilitates Refactoring: With a robust suite of unit tests, developers can refactor code with confidence, knowing that any regressions will be caught by the tests.

2. Writing Unit Tests for API Endpoints

When writing unit tests for API endpoints, it's essential to follow best practices to ensure that the tests are effective and maintainable.

Steps for Writing Unit Tests:

Set Up the Testing Environment: Create a dedicated testing environment that mirrors your production environment. Use a testing framework suitable for your programming language (e.g., JUnit for Java, pytest for Python).

Isolate Dependencies: Use mocking or stubbing techniques to isolate the endpoint being tested from external dependencies, such as databases or third-party services. This isolation helps ensure that tests are focused solely on the functionality of the API endpoint.

Define Test Cases: Clearly define test cases for different scenarios, including:

Valid inputs that should produce expected outputs.

Invalid inputs that should trigger appropriate error responses.

Edge cases that test the boundaries of expected behavior.

Example: Unit Testing an API Endpoint in Node.js

Suppose you have a simple Express API with a /tasks endpoint that retrieves tasks from a database. Here's how you might write a unit test for this endpoint using Mocha and Chai:

javascript

Copy code

const request = require('supertest');

const app = require('../app'); // Your Express app

const chai = require('chai');

```
const expect = chai.expect;
```

```
describe('GET /tasks', () => {

it('should return a list of tasks', (done) => {

request(app)

.get('/tasks')

.expect(200)

.end((err, res) => {

expect(res.body).to.be.an('array');

done();

});

});


it('should return 404 for non-existing endpoint', (done) => {

request(app)

.get('/non-existing-endpoint')

.expect(404, done);

});
```

});

3. Best Practices for Unit Testing

To ensure the effectiveness of your unit tests, consider the following best practices:

Keep Tests Independent: Ensure that tests can be run in isolation without dependencies on other tests. This independence allows for easier identification of failing tests.

Use Descriptive Names: Write descriptive test names that clearly indicate what each test is validating. This clarity aids in understanding the purpose of the tests at a glance.

Run Tests Frequently: Integrate unit tests into your development workflow and run them frequently. This practice helps catch bugs early and maintains code quality.

Tools for Testing APIs: Postman, curl, JUnit

1. Postman

Postman is a popular tool for testing APIs and has become an industry standard for API development. It provides a user-friendly interface for sending requests to your API and inspecting responses.

Key Features of Postman:

Collection Management: Organize your API requests into collections, making it easy to manage related requests.

Environment Variables: Use environment variables to store values like base URLs and API keys, allowing for easy switching between different environments (development, testing, production).

Automated Testing: Postman supports writing test scripts in JavaScript to validate responses automatically.

Example: Testing an API with Postman

Open Postman and create a new request.

Set the request method (GET, POST, etc.) and enter the URL of your API endpoint.

Add any necessary headers, parameters, or request bodies.

Click "Send" to execute the request and view the response.

You can also write test scripts to validate the response:

javascript

Copy code

pm.test("Response should be a JSON object", function () {

pm.response.to.be.json;

```
});
```

pm.test("Response should have a 200 status code", function () {

pm.response.to.have.status(200);

});

2. curl

curl is a command-line tool for transferring data with URLs. It is widely used for testing APIs and can be a powerful option for developers who prefer command-line interfaces.

Key Features of curl:

Flexible Requests: Send various types of HTTP requests (GET, POST, PUT, DELETE) with ease.

Support for Authentication: Easily handle authentication by passing headers or credentials.

Scripting and Automation: Incorporate curl commands into scripts for automated testing.

Example: Using curl to Test an API
To send a GET request using curl, you can use the following command:

bash

Copy code

curl -X GET https://api.example.com/tasks

To send a POST request with JSON data, use:

bash

Copy code

*curl -X POST https://api.example.com/tasks *

*-H "Content-Type: application/json" *

-d '{"title": "New Task", "description": "Task details"}'

3. JUnit

JUnit is a widely used testing framework for Java applications. It provides annotations and assertions to create unit tests easily.
   Key Features of JUnit:

Test Annotations: Use annotations like @Test, @Before, and @After to define test methods and setup/teardown routines.

Assertions: Use assertion methods to verify expected results in your tests.

Integration with Build Tools: JUnit integrates well with build tools like Maven and Gradle, allowing for seamless execution of tests.

Example: Writing Unit Tests with JUnit
Here's an example of how to write a simple unit test for a Java-based API using JUnit and MockMvc:

java

Copy code

import static org.springframework.test.web.servlet.request.Mock-MvcRequestBuilders.get;

import static org.springframework.test.web.servlet.result.Mock-MvcResultMatchers.status;

```
import static org.
springframework.test.web.servlet.
result.MockMvcResult
Matchers.jsonPath;
```

@RunWith(SpringRunner.class)

@WebMvcTest(TaskController.class)

```
public class TaskControllerTest {
```

@Autowired

```
private MockMvc mockMvc;
```

@Test

public void testGetTasks() throws Exception {

mockMvc.perform(get("/tasks"))

.andExpect(status().isOk())

.andExpect(jsonPath("$").isArray());

}

}

Writing Integration Tests for APIs

1. What are Integration Tests?

Integration tests verify that different components of an application work together as expected. In the context of APIs, integration testing focuses on the interaction between the API and external systems, such as databases and third-party services.

Key Benefits of Integration Testing:

Detecting Issues Early: Integration tests help identify issues that may arise when components interact, catching potential bugs before they reach production.

Validating API Functionality: Integration tests ensure that the API endpoints function correctly when integrated with other services and components.

2. Writing Integration Tests for APIs

When writing integration tests for APIs, it's essential to consider the interactions between various components and external systems.

Steps for Writing Integration Tests:

Set Up the Testing Environment: Create a testing environment that mimics production as closely as possible. This setup may include a separate testing database and mock services for external APIs.

Define Test Scenarios: Identify the key scenarios you want to test, including:

Validating that API endpoints correctly interact with the database.

Testing error handling when external services fail.

Ensuring that data is correctly processed and returned.

Example: Integration Testing with Spring Boot

For a Java-based Spring Boot application, you can use Spring's testing support to write integration tests. Here's an example of testing a /tasks endpoint:

java

Copy code

import static org.springframework.boot.test.autoconfigure.web.servlet.AutoConfigureMockMvc;

import static org.springframework.test.web.servlet.request.MockMvcRequestBuilders.post;

```
import static org.springframework.
test.web.servlet.
```

```
result.MockMvcResultMatchers.status;
```

@RunWith(SpringRunner.class)

@SpringBootTest

@AutoConfigureMockMvc

```
public class TaskIntegrationTest {
```

@Autowired

```
private MockMvc mockMvc;
```

@Test

public void testCreateTask() throws Exception {

```
String taskJson = "{\"title\":
\"New Task\", \"description\": \"Task details\"}";
```

mockMvc.perform(post("/tasks")

.contentType(MediaType.APPLICATION_JSON)

```
.content(taskJson))

.andExpect(status().isCreated());

}

}
```

3. Best Practices for Integration

Chapter 8: Securing APIs: Best Practices

As APIs continue to serve as critical components in modern software architecture, the importance of securing these interfaces cannot be overstated. With the rise in cyberattacks targeting APIs, developers and organizations must adopt robust security measures to protect sensitive data and ensure the integrity of their applications. In this chapter, we will explore best practices for securing APIs, focusing on common vulnerabilities, rate limiting, secure communication protocols, and data encryption.

How to Protect Against Common API Vulnerabilities

1. Understanding Common API Vulnerabilities

APIs are susceptible to various vulnerabilities that can be exploited by attackers. Understanding these vulnerabilities is the first step in implementing effective security measures. The most common API vulnerabilities include:

1.1 Injection Attacks

Injection attacks, such as SQL injection, occur when an attacker sends malicious input to an API, exploiting the way the API processes user input. This vulnerability can lead to unauthorized access to databases or execution of arbitrary code.

Example: An API that constructs SQL queries directly from user input without proper validation may allow an attacker to manipulate the SQL query, potentially exposing sensitive data or corrupting the database.

1.2 Cross-Site Scripting (XSS)

XSS vulnerabilities arise when an API includes untrusted data in web pages without proper validation or escaping. Attackers can inject malicious scripts that execute in the context of a user's browser, leading to data theft or unauthorized actions.

Example: An API that returns user-generated content without sanitization may allow an attacker to embed a script that steals cookies or session tokens.

1.3 Denial of Service (DoS) Attacks

DoS attacks aim to make an API or service unavailable to users by over-whelming it with traffic or resource-intensive requests. This vulnerability can disrupt service and degrade performance.

Example: An attacker may flood an API with requests, consuming server resources and preventing legitimate users from accessing the service.

2. Protecting Against Injection Attacks

To safeguard your API against injection attacks, follow these best practices:

2.1 Input Validation and Sanitization

Input Validation: Implement strict input validation to ensure that user input conforms to expected formats. Use whitelisting approaches to allow only known good input and reject anything else.

Input Sanitization: Sanitize user input to remove or escape potentially harmful characters before processing it. For example, use parameterized queries or prepared statements when interacting with databases to prevent SQL injection.

2.2 Use ORM Frameworks

Object-Relational Mapping (ORM): Utilize ORM frameworks, such as Entity Framework or Hibernate, which automatically handle input sanitization and help prevent SQL injection vulnerabilities.

3. Protecting Against Cross-Site Scripting (XSS)

To mitigate XSS vulnerabilities, consider the following strategies:

3.1 Content Security Policy (CSP)

CSP Implementation: Implement a Content Security Policy that specifies which sources of content are allowed to execute on your web pages. This policy helps prevent the execution of malicious scripts.

3.2 Output Encoding

Output Encoding: Encode output data before rendering it in a web page to ensure that any user-generated content is displayed as text rather than executable code. Use libraries like OWASP Java Encoder or Microsoft AntiXSS for this purpose.

4. Protecting Against Denial of Service (DoS) Attacks

To defend against DoS attacks, employ the following practices:

4.1 Rate Limiting

Rate Limiting Implementation: Implement rate limiting to restrict the number of requests a user can make to your API within a specific timeframe. This practice prevents abuse and helps ensure fair usage among users.

4.2 Resource Management

Resource Allocation: Monitor resource consumption and implement resource quotas to limit the impact of potentially malicious requests. Use load balancers to distribute traffic and mitigate the risk of overwhelming a single server.

Implementing Rate Limiting and Throttling

1. Understanding Rate Limiting and Throttling

Rate limiting and throttling are essential techniques for managing API usage and preventing abuse. These methods control the number of requests a client can make within a specified period, ensuring the API remains available for all users.

1.1 Rate Limiting

Rate limiting restricts the number of requests a client can make to an API over a defined time interval. For example, you might limit users to 100 requests per minute.

Benefits of Rate Limiting:

Prevents abuse and protects against DDoS attacks.

Ensures fair usage among clients.

Helps maintain API performance and reliability.

1.2 Throttling

Throttling involves dynamically adjusting the rate limit based on current system load or usage patterns. This method allows you to provide a better user experience by accommodating bursts of legitimate traffic while still protecting the API from abuse.

Example: If the server is experiencing high load, you might temporarily lower the rate limit for all clients or specific users to maintain performance.

2. Implementing Rate Limiting

When implementing rate limiting, consider the following best practices:

2.1 Choose a Rate Limiting Strategy

Fixed Window: Limit requests within fixed time intervals (e.g., 100 requests per minute). This method is straightforward but can lead to burst traffic at the end of each interval.

Sliding Window: Allow a rolling time window that calculates requests over the last minute rather than fixed intervals, providing a smoother experience.

Token Bucket: Use a token bucket algorithm where clients earn tokens at a defined rate, allowing bursts of traffic while enforcing a maximum limit.

2.2 Store Request Counts Efficiently

In-Memory Data Stores: Use in-memory data stores like Redis or Memcached to efficiently store request counts and manage rate limiting.

Database Storage: For persistent rate limiting, store counts in a relational database, ensuring that data is consistent across multiple instances of your API.

2.3 Provide Feedback on Rate Limits

HTTP Headers: Include headers in API responses to communicate rate limit status to clients. Common headers include:

X-RateLimit-Limit: The maximum number of requests allowed.

X-RateLimit-Remaining: The number of requests remaining in the current period.

X-RateLimit-Reset: The time when the rate limit will reset.

Error Responses: Return appropriate error responses (e.g., HTTP 429 Too Many Requests) when clients exceed their rate limits, along with information on when they can make further requests.

Using HTTPS and SSL/TLS for Secure Communication

1. Importance of HTTPS

HTTP Secure (HTTPS) is the foundation of secure communication over the internet. Using HTTPS ensures that data transmitted between clients and servers is encrypted, protecting it from eavesdropping and tampering.
   Key Benefits of HTTPS:

Data Encryption: Encrypts data in transit, preventing attackers from intercepting sensitive information.

Data Integrity: Ensures that data is not altered during transmission.

Authentication: Validates the identity of the server, helping to prevent man-in-the-middle attacks.

2. Implementing SSL/TLS

To implement HTTPS, you must acquire an SSL/TLS certificate and configure your server to use it.

2.1 Obtaining an SSL/TLS Certificate

Choose a Certificate Authority (CA): Select a reputable CA to issue your SSL/TLS certificate. Options include Let's Encrypt (free), DigiCert, and GlobalSign.

Certificate Installation: Follow the CA's instructions for generating a Certificate Signing Request (CSR) and installing the certificate on your web server.

2.2 Configuring Your Server for HTTPS

Web Server Configuration: Configure your web server (e.g., Apache, Nginx) to use the SSL/TLS certificate. This configuration typically involves modifying the server's configuration files to enable HTTPS and redirect HTTP traffic to HTTPS.

HTTP Strict Transport Security (HSTS): Implement HSTS to enforce the use of HTTPS by instructing browsers to only connect to your API over secure connections. This feature mitigates the risk of protocol downgrade attacks.

3. Testing Your HTTPS Configuration

After configuring HTTPS, it's essential to test your implementation to ensure that it is secure.

SSL Labs: Use the SSL Labs SSL Test to analyze your SSL/TLS configuration and receive a grade based on security best practices.

Browser Testing: Access your API using a web browser and inspect the certificate details to ensure that it is valid and trusted.

Data Encryption and Secure Data Transmission

1. Understanding Data Encryption

Data encryption is the process of converting plaintext data into ciphertext to protect it from unauthorized access. In the context of APIs, encryption is crucial for safeguarding sensitive information during transmission and storage.

Key Types of Data Encryption:

Symmetric Encryption: Uses the same key for both encryption and decryption. This method is fast and efficient for encrypting large volumes of data.

Asymmetric Encryption: Uses a pair of keys (public and private) for encryption and decryption. This method is commonly used for secure key exchange.

Chapter 9: API Performance Optimization

Chapter 9: API Performance Optimization

A s the backbone of modern applications, APIs play a crucial role in ensuring seamless communication between different systems and services. However, the performance of APIs can significantly impact user experience and application efficiency. Slow, unresponsive APIs can lead to frustrated users, decreased engagement, and ultimately lost business opportunities. Therefore, optimizing API performance is not just a technical necessity; it is a strategic imperative for any organization.

In this chapter, we will delve into the various aspects of API performance optimization, including understanding its importance, implementing caching strategies, load balancing and scaling APIs for high traffic, and monitoring API performance using various tools. By the end of this chapter, you will have a solid understanding of how to enhance API performance and ensure a smooth user experience.

Understanding the Importance of API Performance

1. Impact on User Experience

API performance directly influences the user experience of applications that rely on these interfaces. Users expect fast, responsive applications, and any delay in API response can lead to frustration and dissatisfaction.

Response Time: Users often have little patience for slow APIs. Research shows that a one-second delay in response time can lead to a significant drop in user satisfaction and conversion rates.

Real-World Example: Consider an e-commerce application. If the API responsible for retrieving product details takes too long to respond, users may abandon their shopping carts and seek alternatives.

2. Business Outcomes

The performance of your API can have far-reaching implications for your business, including:

Customer Retention: High-performing APIs contribute to better customer retention rates. Satisfied users are more likely to return and recommend your services to others.

Revenue Generation: Slow APIs can lead to lost revenue opportunities. For instance, if a payment processing API is slow, users may cancel transactions or choose competitors with faster services.

Operational Efficiency: Optimizing API performance reduces server load, minimizes resource consumption, and enhances overall system efficiency.

3. Competitive Advantage

In a crowded marketplace, performance can be a key differentiator. APIs that provide fast, reliable services can give your organization a competitive edge.

User Trust: High-performing APIs foster trust with users. If your API consistently delivers results quickly, users are more likely to rely on your services.

Scalability: Well-optimized APIs can handle increased traffic and demand without degradation in performance, making it easier to scale your services as your user base grows.

Caching Strategies for APIs

Caching is one of the most effective techniques for optimizing API performance. By storing frequently requested data in a temporary storage location, caching reduces the need to repeatedly fetch data from the primary data source, leading to faster response times.

1. Client-Side Caching

Client-side caching involves storing responses on the client's device, reducing the need for repeated requests to the server.
   Benefits of Client-Side Caching:

Reduced Latency: Retrieving data from the client's cache is faster than making a round-trip to the server, leading to lower latency and improved user experience.

Decreased Server Load: By caching responses on the client side, you reduce the number of requests sent to your API, alleviating load on your server.

Implementation Strategies:

HTTP Caching Headers: Utilize HTTP caching headers to instruct clients on how to cache responses. Common headers include:

Cache-Control: Directs clients on how to cache resources (e.g., public, private, max-age).

Expires: Specifies an expiration date and time for cached resources.

ETag: Provides a unique identifier for a specific version of a resource, allowing clients to validate their cache.

Example:

http

Copy code

Cache-Control: public, max-age=3600

ETag: "abc123"

2. Server-Side Caching

Server-side caching involves storing data on the server to expedite responses to API requests. This approach is particularly useful for APIs that query databases or external services frequently.
  Benefits of Server-Side Caching:

Faster Response Times: Caching responses on the server reduces the time spent retrieving data from slower sources, such as databases.

Improved Resource Efficiency: Server-side caching minimizes the load on databases and other external services, improving overall system performance.

Implementation Strategies:

In-Memory Caching: Use in-memory data stores, such as Redis or Memcached, to cache frequently accessed data. This approach provides rapid access to cached information.

Cache Invalidations: Implement strategies to invalidate cached data when underlying data changes. Common strategies include time-based expiration, manual invalidation, or cache-aside patterns.

Example:

python

Copy code

 # Using Redis for caching in Python

```
import redis

cache = redis.Redis()
```

def get_task(task_id):

cached_task = cache.get(task_id)

if cached_task:

return cached_task

task = fetch_task_from_database(task_id)

cache.set(task_id, task)

return task

3. CDN Caching

Content Delivery Networks (CDNs) cache API responses at edge locations close to users, enhancing performance for geographically distributed applications.

Benefits of CDN Caching:

Reduced Latency: CDNs serve cached content from locations closer to the user, resulting in faster response times.

Load Distribution: By offloading traffic to edge servers, CDNs reduce the load on your origin server, improving scalability.

Implementation Strategies:

CDN Integration: Choose a CDN provider and configure it to cache your API responses. Specify caching rules based on the type of content being served.

Load Balancing and Scaling Your API for High Traffic

As your API gains popularity, it must be capable of handling increased traffic without compromising performance. Load balancing and scaling are essential strategies to achieve this.

1. Understanding Load Balancing

Load balancing distributes incoming API requests across multiple server instances to ensure that no single server becomes overwhelmed. This approach enhances reliability, performance, and fault tolerance.

Types of Load Balancers:

Hardware Load Balancers: Physical devices that manage traffic and distribute requests. They are often used in large enterprises but can be costly.

Software Load Balancers: Applications that run on standard hardware or virtual machines, providing flexibility and cost-effectiveness. Examples include NGINX and HAProxy.

2. Load Balancing Strategies

Choosing the right load balancing strategy is crucial for optimizing API performance:

2.1 Round Robin

Round Robin distributes incoming requests evenly across servers in a rotating manner. Each server receives a request in turn, ensuring even distribution of traffic.

2.2 Least Connections

The Least Connections strategy directs traffic to the server with the fewest active connections. This method is effective for handling varying workloads and ensures that less-busy servers take on new requests.

2.3 IP Hashing

IP Hashing directs requests from the same client IP address to the same server. This strategy can enhance performance by maintaining session state on a single server, but it may lead to uneven load distribution.

3. Horizontal vs. Vertical Scaling

When scaling your API, you can choose between horizontal and vertical scaling:

3.1 Horizontal Scaling

Horizontal scaling involves adding more server instances to distribute the load. This approach is often preferred for APIs, as it enhances fault tolerance and allows for elastic scaling.

Benefits:

Better fault tolerance: If one server fails, others can continue to serve requests.

Scalability: Easily add or remove servers based on demand.

3.2 Vertical Scaling

Vertical scaling entails upgrading existing server hardware (e.g., adding CPU or RAM). While this approach can enhance performance, it has limitations, including a single point of failure.

Drawbacks:

Limited scalability: There's a maximum capacity to which a single server can be upgraded.

Potential downtime: Upgrading may require downtime for the server.

4. Implementing Auto-Scaling

Auto-scaling allows you to automatically adjust the number of server instances based on traffic demand. This capability is essential for handling traffic spikes efficiently.

Key Features of Auto-Scaling:

Threshold-based Scaling: Set thresholds for CPU usage, memory usage, or request counts to trigger scaling actions.

Scheduled Scaling: Configure scaling actions based on predictable traffic patterns (e.g., peak hours).

Monitoring API Performance with Tools

Monitoring is essential for maintaining API performance and identifying potential issues before they impact users. By leveraging monitoring tools, you can gain valuable insights into the health and performance of your APIs.

1. Choosing Monitoring Tools

Several monitoring tools can help you track API performance, including:

1.1 New Relic

New Relic is a comprehensive application performance monitoring (APM) tool that provides real-time insights into application performance.

Key Features:

Real-time monitoring of API response times, error rates, and throughput.

Transaction tracing to identify performance bottlenecks.

Custom dashboards for visualizing key metrics.

1.2 AWS CloudWatch

AWS CloudWatch is a monitoring service for AWS resources and applications. It provides metrics and logs to help monitor API performance.

Key Features:

Custom metrics to track API performance (e.g., request count, error rates).

Alarms and notifications for threshold breaches.

Integration with AWS Lambda and other AWS services for event-driven monitoring.

2. Key Metrics to Monitor

When monitoring API performance, focus on the following key metrics:

2.1 Response Time

Monitor the average response time for API requests to ensure that they meet user expectations. Use tools to track response times over various periods (e.g., hourly, daily) to identify trends.

2.2 Error Rates

Track the rate of errors returned by your API. High error rates may indicate issues with the API or the backend services it relies on.

HTTP Status Codes: Analyze the distribution of HTTP status codes to understand the types of errors occurring (e.g., 4xx for client errors, 5xx for server errors).

2.3 Throughput

Measure the number of requests processed by your API over a specific period. High throughput indicates that your API can handle user demand effectively.

2.4 Latency

Monitor the latency of API requests, including network latency, processing latency, and database latency. Identifying where delays occur can help pinpoint performance bottlenecks.

3. Setting Up Alerts and Notifications

Configuring alerts and notifications based on predefined thresholds is crucial for proactive monitoring. For example:

Response Time Alerts: Set alerts for when response times exceed a certain threshold (e.g., 500ms) to trigger investigations into potential issues.

Error Rate Alerts: Configure alerts for when error rates exceed a specific percentage, indicating potential problems with the API.

Conclusion

In this chapter, we have explored the critical topic of API performance optimization. We discussed the importance of API performance and its impact on user experience and business outcomes. By implementing effective caching strategies, load balancing techniques, and monitoring practices, you can ensure that your API operates reliably and efficiently.

Key Takeaways:

Prioritize Performance: API performance directly impacts user satisfaction and retention. Regularly evaluate and optimize performance to meet user expectations.

Implement Caching: Utilize both client-side and server-side caching strategies to reduce response times and server load.

Load Balance and Scale: Use load balancing and auto-scaling techniques to handle increased traffic and ensure high availability.

Monitor Continuously: Implement monitoring tools to gain insights into API performance and proactively address potential issues.

As you move forward in your API development journey, keep these best practices in mind. By prioritizing performance optimization, you will enhance user experience, improve system reliability, and drive the success of your API-driven applications.

Chapter 10: API Versioning and Backward Compatibility

In the fast-paced world of software development, APIs often evolve to meet changing user needs, incorporate new features, or improve performance. However, with every change, there is the potential for disruption—especially for existing users of the API. This is where API versioning and backward compatibility become critical. Proper versioning ensures that both new and existing users can work with your API without interruption, allowing for ongoing improvements without breaking existing integrations.

In this chapter, we will explore why API versioning is critical, discuss various methods for versioning your API, examine strategies for maintaining backward compatibility, and outline approaches for deprecating old API versions. By the end of this chapter, you will understand how to effectively manage API versioning and ensure a seamless experience for your users.

Why API Versioning Is Critical

1. Managing Changes Without Breaking Functionality

API versioning allows developers to introduce changes to an API while minimizing the risk of breaking existing client applications. When an API is updated—whether by adding new features, modifying existing functionality, or fixing bugs—there's a chance that these changes could disrupt existing integrations.

Example: Consider an e-commerce API that initially provides a simple product retrieval endpoint. If you decide to add additional fields to the product response (e.g., product reviews or ratings), existing clients expecting the original response format may break. By versioning the API, you can introduce the changes in a new version without affecting clients using the old version.

2. Supporting Multiple Client Applications

Different client applications may rely on specific features or behaviors of your API. By implementing versioning, you can support multiple client applications simultaneously, allowing each to use the version of the API that best suits their needs.

Example: A mobile application might rely on an older version of an API due to compatibility concerns. Meanwhile, a web application can adopt the latest version. Versioning enables both applications to coexist, ensuring that users can continue to use your services without disruption.

3. Facilitating Continuous Improvement

Versioning your API allows for continuous improvement and innovation. Developers can introduce new features and enhancements while still supporting legacy applications, fostering an environment of growth and adaptation.

Example: A financial services API might evolve to include new financial products, integrations, or compliance features. By creating new versions, you can enhance the API while maintaining the stability of existing applications.

4. Communicating Changes Clearly

Effective API versioning communicates changes and updates to users clearly. When developers understand which version they are using and what changes have been made in new versions, it fosters transparency and trust.

Example: When releasing a new version of your API, providing detailed release notes that highlight changes, improvements, and potential breaking changes allows users to assess the impact on their applications and plan accordingly.

Methods for Versioning Your API

There are several methods for versioning APIs, each with its own advantages and disadvantages. The choice of versioning method depends on your specific use case and the needs of your API consumers.

1. URI Versioning

URI versioning involves including the version number directly in the API endpoint's URL. This method is straightforward and easy to understand for users.

Example:

plaintext

Copy code

GET /api/v1/products

GET /api/v2/products

Advantages:

Clarity: Including the version number in the URL makes it immediately clear which version of the API is being accessed.

Simplicity: URI versioning is easy to implement and does not require complex server configurations.

Disadvantages:

URL Bloat: As versions increase, the number of endpoints can become unwieldy, leading to potential confusion.

Caching Issues: Caching mechanisms may treat different versions as completely separate resources, which could lead to increased resource usage.

2. Header Versioning

Header versioning involves specifying the API version in the request headers rather than in the URL. This method allows for cleaner URLs and can be more flexible in managing versions.

   Example:

http

Copy code

GET /api/products

Accept: application/vnd.myapi.v1+json

Advantages:

Cleaner URLs: By keeping the version information out of the URL, your endpoints remain clean and focused on resource representation.

Flexibility: You can change the API version without altering the endpoint structure, allowing for more nuanced version management.

Disadvantages:

Less Visibility: Users may not immediately see which version of the API they are using, leading to potential confusion.

Complexity: Implementing header versioning may require additional logic in your API to process and interpret headers.

3. Query Parameter Versioning

Query parameter versioning involves specifying the version in the query string of the API request. This method is less common but can be useful in certain scenarios.

   Example:

plaintext

Copy code

GET /api/products?version=1

Advantages:

Simplicity: Easy to implement, as it does not require complex routing or server configurations.

Clarity: The version information is explicitly stated, making it clear which version is being requested.

Disadvantages:

URL Length: Query parameters can lead to longer URLs, which may be cumbersome for users.

Caching Concerns: Similar to URI versioning, different versions may be treated as separate resources by caching mechanisms.

4. Content Negotiation

Content negotiation allows clients to specify the desired version of the API in the Accept header. This method provides flexibility in how versions are managed and can be combined with other versioning methods.

Example:

http

Copy code

GET /api/products

Accept: application/vnd.myapi.v1+json

Advantages:

Flexibility: Allows clients to specify the desired format and version in a single request.

Cleaner URLs: Like header versioning, content negotiation keeps URLs clean and focused on the resources.

Disadvantages:

Complex Implementation: Requires additional logic to handle content negotiation and version management.

Less Intuitive: Some users may find it less straightforward than URI-based versioning.

Maintaining Backward Compatibility

Backward compatibility is the ability of a new version of an API to coexist with older versions, ensuring that existing clients continue to function without modification. Maintaining backward compatibility is essential for a smooth transition between API versions and for preserving user trust.

1. Design with Compatibility in Mind

When designing a new version of your API, keep backward compatibility in mind from the outset:

1.1 Avoid Breaking Changes

Non-Breaking Changes: When introducing new features or improvements, aim to make changes that do not affect existing functionality. For example, adding new fields to a response object is generally non-breaking, as clients that do not expect the new fields will continue to function correctly.

Deprecation Strategy: If breaking changes are unavoidable, implement a clear deprecation strategy. Notify users well in advance and provide guidance on how to migrate to the new version.

1.2 Versioned Documentation

Documentation Clarity: Provide clear documentation for both the current and deprecated versions of your API. This helps users understand changes and how to adapt their applications accordingly.

2. Testing for Backward Compatibility

Regular testing is crucial for ensuring backward compatibility between API versions. Here are some strategies for testing:

2.1 Regression Testing

Automated Tests: Implement automated tests that cover existing functionality and validate that new changes do not introduce regressions. This includes unit tests, integration tests, and end-to-end tests.

Continuous Integration (CI): Integrate regression tests into your CI pipeline to ensure that every new version is validated against existing tests.

2.2 User Acceptance Testing (UAT)

Involve Users: Engage users in testing the new version of the API. Gather feedback on their experiences and address any compatibility issues that arise.

Strategies for Deprecating Old API Versions

Deprecating old API versions is a natural part of the API lifecycle. As new versions are introduced, it's essential to manage the deprecation process carefully to minimize disruption for users.

1. Clear Communication

Effective communication is key to a smooth deprecation process. Consider the following strategies:

1.1 Advance Notice

Notify Users Early: Inform users of the upcoming deprecation well in advance. Provide details about the timeline for deprecation and the reasons for the change.

Documentation Updates: Update your documentation to reflect the deprecation, including guidance on migrating to the new version.

1.2 Multiple Channels of Communication

Email Notifications: Send email notifications to registered users and stakeholders about the deprecation timeline.

In-App Messages: If applicable, implement in-app notifications or banners to inform users about the deprecation when they access the old version.

2. Providing Migration Support

Supporting users through the migration process is essential for maintaining trust and satisfaction. Here are some strategies:

2.1 Migration Guides

Detailed Documentation: Create detailed migration guides that outline the changes between versions, highlight any breaking changes, and provide code examples for migrating to the new version.

2.2 API Versioning in Documentation

Versioned Documentation: Maintain versioned documentation for both the old and new API versions. This ensures that users can reference the documentation that corresponds to the version they are using.

3. Implementing Graceful Degradation

During the deprecation process, consider implementing graceful degradation to support users who have not yet migrated.

3.1 Grace Periods

Maintain Old Versions Temporarily: Allow the old version to remain operational for a specified grace period after the initial deprecation announcement. This gives users time to migrate to the new version without immediate disruption.

3.2 Redirects and Error Handling

Redirection: If feasible, implement redirects from the old endpoint to the new endpoint. This can help users transition smoothly to the new version.

Custom Error Messages: When users access deprecated endpoints, return custom error messages that inform them of the deprecation and provide links to the new version and migration resources.

Conclusion

In this chapter, we have explored the critical topics of API versioning and backward compatibility. We discussed why versioning is essential, the various methods for implementing versioning, strategies for maintaining backward compatibility, and approaches for deprecating old API versions.

Key Takeaways:

Prioritize Versioning: Implement API versioning from the outset to manage changes effectively and support multiple client applications.

Choose the Right Method: Select a versioning method that aligns with your API's needs and provides clarity for users.

Communicate Clearly: Provide clear communication about changes, deprecations, and migration paths to maintain user trust.

Support Migration: Offer comprehensive migration guides and support to help users transition to new API versions smoothly.

As you continue your API development journey, remember that effective versioning and backward compatibility are essential for maintaining a reliable, user-friendly API. By following the best practices outlined in this chapter, you can ensure a seamless experience for your users and foster long-term success for your API.

Chapter 11: API Rate Limiting and Throttling

In the rapidly evolving landscape of web development, APIs serve as critical gateways for data exchange between applications and services. However, with the increased adoption of APIs comes the potential for abuse, whether intentional or accidental. Rate limiting and throttling are essential techniques for controlling the flow of traffic to your API, ensuring that it remains responsive and secure while protecting it from various threats. In this chapter, we will delve into the significance of rate limiting, explore how to implement it using middleware, discuss setting up throttling and quotas for high-traffic APIs, and examine real-world examples from industry leaders like Stripe and Twitter.

Why Rate Limiting Matters for API Security

1. Protecting Against Abuse and Overuse

Rate limiting serves as a critical defense mechanism against various forms of abuse, including:

1.1 Denial of Service (DoS) Attacks

In a Denial of Service attack, an attacker attempts to overwhelm an API by flooding it with requests, causing it to become unresponsive or crash. Rate limiting can help mitigate the impact of such attacks by capping the number of requests a single user or IP address can make in a given timeframe.

- **Example**: If an attacker attempts to send 1,000 requests per second, a properly configured rate limiting system can restrict them to, say, 10 requests per second, effectively thwarting the attack.

1.2 Resource Exhaustion

High volumes of requests can lead to resource exhaustion, where servers become overloaded and unable to process legitimate requests. Rate limiting helps ensure that your API can continue to serve its intended users by limiting the number of requests from any single source.

- **Example**: If an API is designed to handle a maximum of 100 requests per second, allowing a single user to exceed this limit could lead to degraded performance or outages for all users.

2. Ensuring Fair Usage

Rate limiting promotes fair usage of your API by preventing any single user from monopolizing resources. This is particularly important for APIs that serve multiple clients or users.

- **Example**: In a public API, rate limiting ensures that no single user can exhaust the available bandwidth or processing power, allowing all users to benefit from the service.

3. Improving API Performance

By controlling the rate of incoming requests, you can help maintain consistent API performance. This consistency leads to faster response times and a better overall user experience.

- **Example**: A travel booking API may implement rate limiting to prevent excessive search queries from overwhelming its backend systems, ensuring that legitimate users can quickly obtain search results without delay.

4. Protecting Sensitive Data

APIs often handle sensitive data, making them attractive targets for malicious actors. Rate limiting can serve as an additional layer of security, reducing the likelihood of unauthorized access attempts.

- **Example**: An API that provides access to user profiles might enforce rate limits to prevent attackers from brute-forcing access to user accounts.

Implementing Rate Limiting Using Middleware

1. Understanding Middleware

Middleware is software that acts as an intermediary between different components of an application. In the context of APIs, middleware can be used to intercept incoming requests and apply rate limiting logic before the requests reach the main application.

2. Choosing a Middleware Library

Various middleware libraries are available for different programming languages and frameworks. When selecting a rate limiting middleware, consider factors such as ease of use, configurability, and compatibility with your existing setup.

Examples of Popular Middleware Libraries:

- **Express-rate-limit** (Node.js): A simple rate limiting middleware for Express applications.

- **Flask-Limiter** (Python): A flexible rate limiting extension for Flask applications.
- **RateLimit** (Ruby on Rails): A rate limiting solution for Rails applications.

3. Implementing Rate Limiting in Express (Node.js)

Here's a step-by-step guide to implementing rate limiting using the express-rate-limit library in a Node.js application.

Step 1: Install the Library

Install the express-rate-limit package using npm:

```bash
Copy code
npm install express-rate-limit
```

Step 2: Configure Rate Limiting

Create a rate limiter instance and configure the desired rate limit settings. For example, you may want to limit requests to 100 per 15 minutes:

```javascript
Copy code
const rateLimit = require('express-rate-limit');

const limiter = rateLimit({
  windowMs: 15 * 60 * 1000, // 15 minutes
  max: 100, // limit each IP to 100 requests per windowMs
  message: 'Too many requests, please try again later.'
});
```

Step 3: Apply the Rate Limiter to Routes

Apply the rate limiter to specific routes or globally to all routes in your application:

```javascript
javascript
Copy code
const express = require('express');
const app = express();

// Apply the rate limiter to all requests
app.use(limiter);

// Example route
app.get('/api/products', (req, res) => {
  res.send('Product list');
});

const PORT = process.env.PORT || 3000;
app.listen(PORT, () => {
  console.log(`Server running on port ${PORT}`);
});
```

4. Implementing Rate Limiting in Flask (Python)

Here's how to implement rate limiting in a Flask application using the Flask-Limiter extension.

Step 1: Install Flask-Limiter

Install the Flask-Limiter package using pip:

```bash
bash
Copy code
pip install Flask-Limiter
```

Step 2: Configure Flask-Limiter

Set up the Flask-Limiter in your Flask application:

```python
python
Copy code
```

```
from flask import Flask
from flask_limiter import Limiter

app = Flask(__name__)
limiter = Limiter(app, key_func=get_remote_address)  # You can
customize key_func to use a different method for identifying
clients.
```

Step 3: Apply Rate Limits to Routes
You can apply rate limits to specific routes using decorators:

```python
Copy code
@app.route('/api/products')
@limiter.limit("100 per 15 minutes")  # Limit to 100 requests per
15 minutes
def get_products():
    return 'Product list'

if __name__ == '__main__':
    app.run(port=5000)
```

Setting Up Throttling and Quotas for High Traffic APIs

1. Understanding Throttling

Throttling is a mechanism that controls the rate of requests that users can make to an API. It helps ensure that your API can handle traffic spikes without degrading performance.

2. Implementing Throttling

2.1 Rate Limiting vs. Throttling
While rate limiting typically restricts the number of requests over a specific time period, throttling can involve more dynamic adjustments based on the

current load and usage patterns. For example, you may choose to temporarily lower the rate limits for all users if your API is experiencing high traffic.

2.2 Throttling Strategies

- **Fixed Rate Throttling**: Set fixed limits on the number of requests per user or IP address within a defined time window.
- **Dynamic Throttling**: Adjust throttling limits based on server load or traffic patterns. For example, during peak hours, you might reduce the allowed request rate to ensure consistent performance for all users.

3. Setting Up Quotas

Quotas are limits on the total number of requests a user can make over an extended period (e.g., daily, monthly). Quotas are often used in combination with rate limiting and throttling.

Benefits of Quotas:

- **Predictable Resource Allocation**: Quotas help manage resource allocation, ensuring that users do not exceed predefined limits.
- **Encouraging Fair Usage**: Quotas promote fair usage of resources among all users, preventing any single user from monopolizing the API.

4. Implementing Quotas in Your API

4.1 Tracking User Usage

To implement quotas, you need to track the usage of each user or client. This can be done using a database or an in-memory data store like Redis.

4.2 Example Implementation

Here's a basic example of implementing quotas in a Node.js application using an in-memory store:

```javascript
Copy code
const express = require('express');
const app = express();

const quotas = {}; // In-memory store for user quotas

app.use((req, res, next) => {
  const userId = req.ip; // Identify user by IP (use a better
  method for production)

  // Initialize user quota if not already set
  if (!quotas[userId]) {
    quotas[userId] = { requests: 0, resetTime: Date.now() + 24 *
    60 * 60 * 1000 }; // 24-hour reset
  }

  // Check if the quota has been exceeded
  if (Date.now() > quotas[userId].resetTime) {
    quotas[userId].requests = 0; // Reset the quota
    quotas[userId].resetTime = Date.now() + 24 * 60 * 60 * 1000;
    // Reset time for next 24 hours
  }

  quotas[userId].requests++;

  if (quotas[userId].requests > 1000) { // Limit to 1000 requests
  per 24 hours
    return res.status(429).json({ message: 'Quota exceeded. Try
    again later.' });
  }

  next();
});

app.get('/api/products', (req, res) => {
  res.send('Product list');
});

const PORT = process.env.PORT || 3000;
```

```
app.listen(PORT, () => {
  console.log(`Server running on port ${PORT}`);
});
```

Real-World Examples of Rate Limiting

1. Stripe API

Stripe is a popular payment processing platform that utilizes rate limiting to ensure fair usage and protect its resources.

Stripe's Rate Limiting Policies:

- **Standard Rate Limits**: Stripe imposes standard rate limits for its API endpoints, generally allowing up to 100 requests per second for most endpoints.
- **Dynamic Rate Limits**: For endpoints that handle more significant resource usage (e.g., creating charges), Stripe may enforce lower limits to maintain performance.
- **Response Headers**: Stripe includes headers in its responses to inform clients of their current usage and remaining requests. For example, headers like X-RateLimit-Limit, X-RateLimit-Remaining, and X-RateLimit-Reset provide valuable insights into rate limiting.

2. Twitter API

Twitter's API is another example of effective rate limiting and throttling. Given the vast number of users and the high volume of requests, Twitter employs strict rate limiting to manage traffic and ensure service availability.

Twitter's Rate Limiting Policies:

- **Rate Limit Windows**: Twitter uses rate limit windows that define how many requests users can make within specific time frames (e.g.,

15 minutes).

- **Per-Endpoint Limits**: Different endpoints have different rate limits based on their resource consumption. For example, the statuses/update endpoint has a lower limit compared to the statuses/user_timeline endpoint.
- **HTTP Status Codes**: When a user exceeds their rate limit, Twitter responds with an HTTP 429 status code (Too Many Requests), accompanied by information about when they can make requests again.

3. Google Maps API

The Google Maps API uses a combination of rate limiting and quotas to manage usage effectively.
Google Maps API Rate Limiting:

- **Daily Quotas**: Google Maps sets daily quotas for API usage based on the pricing plan selected by the user. This ensures that users stay within their limits and manage costs effectively.
- **Per-Project Limits**: Google imposes limits at the project level, so all requests made from a specific project contribute to a single quota.
- **Dynamic Pricing**: Google's API pricing model is based on usage, and exceeding quotas can lead to increased costs, encouraging developers to optimize their API calls.

Conclusion

In this chapter, we explored the essential topic of API rate limiting and throttling. We discussed why rate limiting matters for API security, how to implement rate limiting using middleware, strategies for setting up throttling and quotas for high-traffic APIs, and real-world examples of effective rate limiting from industry leaders like Stripe, Twitter, and Google Maps.

Key Takeaways:

- **Prioritize Security**: Rate limiting is crucial for protecting your API against abuse, ensuring fair usage, and maintaining performance.
- **Implement Middleware**: Use middleware to easily apply rate limiting and throttling to your API endpoints.
- **Track Usage**: Monitor user usage effectively to enforce quotas and ensure fair access to resources.
- **Learn from Real-World Examples**: Study successful implementations of rate limiting by industry leaders to inform your strategies.

As you continue your journey in API development, remember that implementing effective rate limiting and throttling practices is essential for building secure, reliable, and high-performing APIs. By following the best practices outlined in this chapter, you can enhance your API's security and improve the overall user experience.

Chapter 12: Exploring GraphQL vs. REST

Chapter 12: Exploring GraphQL vs. REST

APIs are a cornerstone of modern application development, facilitating communication between client and server systems. Among the various API architectures, REST (Representational State Transfer) and GraphQL have emerged as two dominant paradigms, each with its own advantages and use cases. Understanding the differences between REST and GraphQL, as well as the contexts in which each should be employed, is crucial for developers looking to create efficient, scalable APIs.

In this chapter, we will explore the key differences between REST and GraphQL, analyze the pros and cons of using GraphQL, walk through the process of building a simple GraphQL API, and provide guidance on when to choose REST over GraphQL and vice versa. By the end of this chapter, you will have a comprehensive understanding of both technologies and be well-equipped to make informed decisions for your API development projects.

Differences Between REST and GraphQL

1. Architectural Style

1.1 REST

REST is an architectural style that uses standard HTTP methods (GET, POST, PUT, DELETE) to perform operations on resources, which are identified by unique URIs (Uniform Resource Identifiers). RESTful APIs adhere to a stateless client-server model, where each request from a client must contain all the information necessary to understand and process the request.

Resource-Oriented: REST APIs are centered around resources. Each resource is represented by a unique URI, and the API exposes endpoints that allow clients to interact with these resources.

Statelessness: Each API call is independent, meaning that the server does not retain any client context between requests.

1.2 GraphQL

GraphQL is a query language for APIs developed by Facebook that provides a more flexible and efficient approach to interacting with data. Unlike REST, where the server defines the structure of the responses, GraphQL allows clients to specify the shape of the data they need.

Flexible Queries: Clients can request exactly the data they need and nothing more, reducing over-fetching and under-fetching of data.

Single Endpoint: GraphQL typically uses a single endpoint for all queries and mutations, simplifying the API structure.

2. Data Fetching

2.1 REST

In REST, fetching data often requires multiple requests to different endpoints to retrieve related resources. This can lead to issues such as over-fetching (retrieving more data than needed) or under-fetching (not retrieving enough data in a single request).

Example: To fetch a user's profile and their associated posts, a client may need to make two separate requests to /users/{id} and /users/{id}/posts.

2.2 GraphQL

With GraphQL, clients can request multiple related resources in a single query, specifying exactly what data they need. This capability reduces the number of requests required to fetch related data.

Example: A client can fetch a user's profile and their posts in one query:

graphql

Copy code

{

user(id: "1") {

name

email

posts {

title

content

}

}

}

3. Versioning

3.1 REST

Versioning is a common practice in REST APIs to manage changes over time. API providers often implement versioning by creating new endpoints for each version (e.g., /v1/users, /v2/users).

Drawbacks: Managing multiple versions can lead to increased complexity and maintenance overhead.

3.2 GraphQL

GraphQL APIs can evolve without the need for versioning. Since clients can request only the data they need, the schema can be modified without breaking existing queries.

Schema Evolution: Adding new fields or types to a GraphQL schema does not affect existing queries, making it easier to manage changes over time.

4. Error Handling

4.1 REST

REST APIs typically rely on standard HTTP status codes to indicate the success or failure of a request. For example, a 200 OK status indicates success, while a 404 Not Found indicates that the requested resource could not be found.

4.2 GraphQL

In GraphQL, errors are returned in the response body alongside the requested data. Even if part of a query fails, the response will still include the successful data and a list of errors.

Example:

json

Copy code

{

"data": {

"user": null

},

"errors": [

```
{

"message": "User not found",

"locations": [{ "line": 1, "column": 2}]

}

]

}
```

Pros and Cons of Using GraphQL

1. Pros of GraphQL

1.1 Flexibility in Data Retrieval
GraphQL provides clients with the flexibility to request precisely the data they need, reducing over-fetching and under-fetching.

Efficiency: Clients can optimize their queries based on their specific requirements, leading to more efficient data retrieval.

1.2 Single Endpoint for Queries
With GraphQL, there is no need to manage multiple endpoints for different resources. This simplicity can lead to cleaner and more maintainable APIs.

Reduced Complexity: A single endpoint simplifies routing and reduces the overhead of managing multiple URLs.

1.3 Strongly Typed Schema
GraphQL uses a strongly typed schema that defines the types and relationships between data. This schema serves as both documentation and a contract between the client and server.

Enhanced Validation: The strong typing allows for better validation of requests and provides tools for automatic documentation generation.

1.4 Built-In Documentation
GraphQL APIs often provide tools like GraphiQL or Apollo Studio, which offer interactive documentation and an intuitive interface for exploring the API.

Improved Developer Experience: Developers can easily test queries and view documentation directly in the interface, making it easier to integrate with the API.

2. Cons of GraphQL

2.1 Complexity of Implementation
Implementing a GraphQL API can be more complex than a RESTful API, especially for developers who are unfamiliar with the paradigm.

Learning Curve: Developers must learn the syntax of GraphQL, as well as how to structure queries and mutations effectively.

2.2 Performance Overhead

While GraphQL can reduce over-fetching, it may lead to performance overhead if clients request deeply nested resources that require extensive processing.

Potential for Inefficiency: Complex queries can result in performance issues if not managed properly, especially when retrieving large data sets.

2.3 Caching Challenges

Caching responses can be more challenging in GraphQL due to the dynamic nature of queries. Since clients can request any combination of fields, traditional caching mechanisms may not be as effective.

Custom Caching Solutions: Implementing effective caching strategies for GraphQL may require custom solutions, which can add complexity.

Building a Simple GraphQL API

1. Setting Up Your Environment

To build a simple GraphQL API, you need to set up your development environment. For this example, we'll use Node.js with Express and Apollo Server.

Step 1: Install Dependencies

Create a new directory for your project and navigate to it in your terminal. Then run the following commands:

bash

Copy code

mkdir graphql-api

cd graphql-api

npm init -y

npm install express apollo-server-express graphql

2. Defining Your GraphQL Schema

In GraphQL, you define a schema that describes the types and structure of your data. Create a new file named schema.js and define your types.

javascript

Copy code

// schema.js

```
const { gql } = require('apollo-server-express');
```

const typeDefs = gql'

type Product {

id: ID!

name: String!

price: Float!

}

type Query {

products: [Product]

product(id: ID!): Product

}

`;

module.exports = typeDefs;

3. Implementing Resolvers

Resolvers are functions that handle the logic for fetching data. Create a new file named resolvers.js and implement your resolvers.

javascript

Copy code

```
// resolvers.js

const products = [

{ id: '1', name: 'Product A', price: 29.99 },

{ id: '2', name: 'Product B', price: 49.99 },

{ id: '3', name: 'Product C', price: 19.99 },


];


const resolvers = {

Query: {
```

products: () => products,

product: (parent, args) => products.find(product => product.id ===
args.id),

},

* };*

module.exports = resolvers;

4. Setting Up the Apollo Server

Create a new file named server.js to set up the Apollo Server and integrate it
with Express.

javascript

Copy code

// server.js

const express = require('express');

const { ApolloServer } = require('apollo-server-express');

const typeDefs = require('./schema');

```
const resolvers = require('./resolvers');
```

const app = express();

```
const server = new ApolloServer({ typeDefs, resolvers });

server.applyMiddleware({ app });
```

const PORT = process.env.PORT || 4000;

app.listen(PORT, () => {

console.log(' Server ready at http://localhost:${PORT}${server.graphqlPath}');

});

5. Running Your GraphQL API

To run your GraphQL API, execute the following command in your terminal:

bash

Copy code

node server.js

You should see a message indicating that the server is running. You can then navigate to http://localhost:4000/graphql in your browser to access the GraphQL playground, where you can test your queries.

6. Testing Your GraphQL API

Using the GraphQL playground, you can test your API with queries such as:

Fetching All Products:

graphql

Copy code

```
{

products {

id

name

price

}

}
```

Fetching a Single Product by ID:

graphql

Copy code

```
{
```

```
product(id: "1") {

id

name

price

}

}
```

When to Choose REST Over GraphQL and Vice Versa

Choosing between REST and GraphQL depends on various factors, including the specific use case, team expertise, and the nature of the application. Here are some considerations to help you decide when to use each approach.

1. When to Choose REST

1.1 Simplicity of Use Cases
REST is often the better choice for simpler use cases where the API interactions are straightforward and predictable. For example, applications that primarily perform CRUD operations on resources may benefit from the simplicity of REST.

Example: A basic blogging platform with endpoints for creating, reading, updating, and deleting blog posts.

1.2 Established Conventions

REST has been around for a long time and is well understood by developers. If your team is already familiar with RESTful practices and conventions, it may be more efficient to stick with what you know.

Example: If your organization has a long history of building REST APIs, migrating to GraphQL might introduce unnecessary complexity.

1.3 Cache-Friendly Operations

RESTful APIs leverage standard HTTP caching mechanisms more easily than GraphQL APIs, which can lead to better performance for cacheable resources.

Example: Public APIs that return static resources, such as images or articles, can benefit from standard HTTP caching.

2. When to Choose GraphQL

2.1 Complex Data Requirements

If your application requires complex data relationships or involves multiple nested resources, GraphQL is often a better choice. GraphQL allows clients to specify precisely what data they need, reducing over-fetching and improving efficiency.

Example: A social media application that retrieves user profiles, posts, and comments can benefit from GraphQL's ability to fetch multiple related resources in a single request.

2.2 Rapid Iteration and Development

GraphQL's flexible nature allows for rapid iteration and development. If you anticipate frequent changes to your API or need to accommodate evolving client requirements, GraphQL can provide the flexibility you need.

Example: A startup building a mobile application may need to iterate quickly based on user feedback, making GraphQL a suitable choice for adapting to changing requirements.

2.3 Strongly Typed Schema and Documentation

GraphQL's strongly typed schema serves as a self-documenting feature, making it easier for developers to understand the API's structure. If you prioritize strong type validation and documentation, GraphQL can enhance the developer experience.

Example: Large teams working on complex applications can benefit from the clarity provided by GraphQL's schema, reducing misunderstandings and improving collaboration.

Conclusion

In this chapter, we explored the critical comparison between GraphQL and REST, highlighting their differences, advantages, and disadvantages. We discussed the flexibility of GraphQL in data retrieval, the simplicity of REST for straightforward use cases, and the importance of understanding when to choose one over the other.

Key Takeaways:

API Design Choices: Understanding the strengths and weaknesses of both GraphQL and REST is essential for making informed design choices.

Flexibility vs. Simplicity: Choose GraphQL for complex data interactions that require flexibility, while REST may be more suitable for simpler, CRUD-focused applications.

Implementation Matters: The choice of API technology should align with your project requirements, team expertise, and anticipated future changes.

As you continue your API development journey, consider the factors discussed in this chapter to make the best choice for your specific use case. By leveraging the strengths of either GraphQL or REST, you can create APIs that effectively meet the needs of your applications and users.

Chapter 13: Real-World API Development with Popular Frameworks

I n the modern world of software development, APIs are essential for creating scalable and efficient applications. With a myriad of frameworks available, developers have the flexibility to choose the best tools for their projects. This chapter will explore API development using three popular frameworks: Express.js for Node.js, Flask for Python, and ASP.NET Core for C#. We will delve into each framework's strengths, walk through practical examples of building APIs, and provide guidance on selecting the most suitable framework for your needs.

Introduction to API Development with Express.js (Node.js)

1. Understanding Express.js

Express.js is a minimal and flexible web application framework for Node.js, designed to simplify the development of web applications and APIs. Its unopinionated nature allows developers to structure their applications as they see fit, making it a popular choice for building APIs.

Key Features of Express.js:

Lightweight and Fast: Express is designed to be minimal and efficient, enabling quick development of web applications and APIs.

Middleware Support: Express uses middleware functions to handle requests, allowing developers to add functionality to their applications easily.

Routing: Express provides a powerful routing system, making it easy to define endpoints and manage requests.

2. Setting Up Your Express.js Environment

To get started with Express.js, you'll need to set up your development environment. Here's how to do it step by step:

Step 1: Install Node.js

Ensure that Node.js is installed on your system. You can download it from the official Node.js website.

Step 2: Create a New Project

Create a new directory for your project and navigate to it in your terminal:

bash

Copy code

mkdir express-api

cd express-api

npm init -y

Step 3: Install Express
Install Express and any other necessary packages:

bash

Copy code

npm install express

3. Building a Simple API with Express.js

Now that your environment is set up, let's build a simple API that manages a collection of products.

Step 1: Create the Main Application File
Create a new file named app.js and set up a basic Express server:

javascript

Copy code

// app.js

const express = require('express');

const app = express();

```
const PORT = process.env.PORT || 3000;
```

// Middleware to parse JSON requests

```
app.use(express.json());
```

// Sample product data

const products = [

{ id: 1, name: 'Product A', price: 29.99 },

{ id: 2, name: 'Product B', price: 49.99 },

```
];
```

// GET endpoint to retrieve all products

app.get('/api/products', (req, res) => {

res.json(products);

```
});
```

// GET endpoint to retrieve a single product by ID

app.get('/api/products/:id', (req, res) => {

```
const product = products.find(p => p.id === parseInt(req.params.id));

if (!product) return res.status(404).send('Product not found');

res.json(product);


});


// POST endpoint to create a new product

app.post('/api/products', (req, res) => {

const { name, price } = req.body;

const newProduct = { id: products.length + 1, name, price };

products.push(newProduct);

res.status(201).json(newProduct);


});


// Start the server

app.listen(PORT, () => {

console.log(`Server running on port ${PORT}`);
```

});

4. Testing Your Express API

To test your API, use a tool like Postman or cURL.
Testing with Postman:

GET All Products: Send a GET request to http://localhost:3000/api/products.

GET Single Product: Send a GET request to http://localhost:3000/api/products/1.

POST New Product: Send a POST request to http://localhost:3000/api/products with a JSON body:

json

Copy code

{

"name": "Product C",

"price": 19.99

}

5. Adding Middleware for Security

To enhance the security of your API, you can add middleware for logging, authentication, and error handling. Here's how to implement some basic security practices:

Step 1: Install Additional Packages

Install helmet for securing HTTP headers:

bash

Copy code

npm install helmet

Step 2: Use Helmet Middleware

Update your app.js file to include Helmet:

javascript

Copy code

```
const helmet = require('helmet');
```

// Use Helmet for basic security

app.use(helmet());

Building APIs with Flask (Python)

1. Understanding Flask

Flask is a micro web framework for Python, known for its simplicity and ease of use. It is lightweight, flexible, and allows developers to quickly build web applications and APIs.

Key Features of Flask:

Minimalist: Flask is designed to keep the core simple while allowing developers to extend functionality as needed.

Built-in Development Server: Flask comes with a built-in server for quick testing and development.

Flexible Routing: Flask allows for easy routing and supports RESTful practices out of the box.

2. Setting Up Your Flask Environment

To get started with Flask, you need to set up your development environment.
Step 1: Install Flask
You can install Flask using pip. Create a virtual environment for your project:

bash

Copy code

mkdir flask-api

cd flask-api

python -m venv venv

source venv/bin/activate # On Windows, use 'venv\Scripts\activate'

pip install Flask

3. Building a Simple API with Flask

Let's create a simple API that manages a collection of products using Flask.

Step 1: Create the Main Application File

Create a new file named app.py and set up a basic Flask server:

python

Copy code

 # app.py

```
from flask import Flask, jsonify, request

app = Flask(__name__)
```

 # Sample product data

products = [

{"id": 1, "name": "Product A", "price": 29.99},

{"id": 2, "name": "Product B", "price": 49.99},

]

 # GET endpoint to retrieve all products

```
@app.route('/api/products', methods=['GET'])

def get_products():

    return jsonify(products)
```

```
# GET endpoint to retrieve a single product by ID

@app.route('/api/products/<int:id>', methods=['GET'])

def get_product(id):

product = next((p for p in products if p['id'] == id), None)

if product is None:

return jsonify({"error": "Product not found"}), 404

    return jsonify(product)
```

```
# POST endpoint to create a new product

@app.route('/api/products', methods=['POST'])

def create_product():

new_product = request.get_json()
```

new_product['id'] = len(products) + 1

products.append(new_product)

```
    return jsonify(new_product), 201
```

if __name__ == '__main__':

app.run(debug=True)

4. Testing Your Flask API

Similar to Express, you can test your Flask API using Postman or cURL.
Testing with Postman:

GET All Products: Send a GET request to http://localhost:5000/api/products.

GET Single Product: Send a GET request to http://localhost:5000/api/products/1.

POST New Product: Send a POST request to http://localhost:5000/api/products with a JSON body:

json

Copy code

{

"name": "Product C",

"price": 19.99

}

5. Adding Middleware for Security

Flask allows you to use middleware to enhance security. Here are some practices:

Step 1: Install Flask-Cors

For handling Cross-Origin Resource Sharing (CORS), install Flask-CORS:

bash

Copy code

pip install flask-cors

Step 2: Use Flask-CORS

Update your app.py to enable CORS:

python

Copy code

```
from flask_cors import CORS
```

 # Enable CORS for all routes

CORS(app)

Creating Secure APIs with ASP.NET Core (C#)

1. Understanding ASP.NET Core

ASP.NET Core is a robust, cross-platform framework for building web applications and APIs. It provides a powerful, feature-rich environment that supports modern development practices.

Key Features of ASP.NET Core:

Cross-Platform: ASP.NET Core runs on Windows, macOS, and Linux, allowing developers to build APIs on any platform.

Dependency Injection: Built-in support for dependency injection enhances testability and maintainability.

Middleware Pipeline: ASP.NET Core uses a middleware pipeline that allows developers to configure request processing.

2. Setting Up Your ASP.NET Core Environment

To get started with ASP.NET Core, ensure you have the .NET SDK installed on your machine.

Step 1: Create a New Project

Create a new ASP.NET Core Web API project using the .NET CLI:

bash

Copy code

dotnet new webapi -n AspNetCoreApi

cd AspNetCoreApi

Step 2: Restore Dependencies
Run the following command to restore any dependencies:

bash

Copy code

dotnet restore

3. Building a Simple API with ASP.NET Core

Let's create a simple API that manages a collection of products.
Step 1: Modify the Model
In the Models folder, create a new file named Product.cs:

csharp

Copy code

// Models/Product.cs

public class Product

{

public int Id { get; set; }

public string Name { get; set; }

public decimal Price { get; set; }

}

Step 2: Create a Controller
In the Controllers folder, create a new file named ProductsController.cs:

csharp

Copy code

// Controllers/ProductsController.cs

using Microsoft.AspNetCore.Mvc;

using System.Collections.Generic;

```
using System.Linq;
```

[ApiController]

[Route("api/[controller]")]

public class ProductsController : ControllerBase

{

```
private static List<Product> products = new List<Product>

{

new Product { Id = 1, Name = "Product A", Price = 29.99M },

new Product { Id = 2, Name = "Product B", Price = 49.99M }

};


[HttpGet]

public ActionResult<IEnumerable<Product>> GetProducts()

{

return Ok(products);

}


[HttpGet("{id}")]

public ActionResult<Product> GetProduct(int id)

{

var product = products.FirstOrDefault(p => p.Id == id);
```

```
if (product == null) return NotFound();

return Ok(product);

    }


[HttpPost]

public ActionResult<Product> CreateProduct(Product product)

{

product.Id = products.Count + 1;

products.Add(product);

return CreatedAtAction(nameof(GetProduct), new { id = product.Id },
product);

}

}
```

4. Running Your ASP.NET Core API

To run your ASP.NET Core API, execute the following command in your terminal:

bash

Copy code

dotnet run

Your API should now be running on http://localhost:5000/api/products.

5. Testing Your ASP.NET Core API

Use Postman or cURL to test your API.
   Testing with Postman:

GET All Products: Send a GET request to http://localhost:5000/api/products.

GET Single Product: Send a GET request to http://localhost:5000/api/products/1.

POST New Product: Send a POST request to http://localhost:5000/api/products with a JSON body:

json

Copy code

{

"name": "Product C",

"price": 19.99

}

6. Adding Middleware for Security

ASP.NET Core provides various middleware for enhancing API security.

Step 1: Install NuGet Packages

You may want to install packages for authentication and authorization, such as:

bash

Copy code

dotnet add package Microsoft.AspNetCore.Authentication.JwtBearer

Step 2: Configure Security in Startup.cs

In the Startup.cs file, configure authentication and authorization middleware:

csharp

Copy code

public void ConfigureServices(IServiceCollection services)

{

services.AddAuthentication(JwtBearerDefaults.Authentication-Scheme)

.AddJwtBearer(options =>

{

```
options.TokenValidationParameters = new
TokenValidationParameters

{

ValidateIssuer = true,

ValidateAudience = true,

ValidateLifetime = true,

ValidateIssuerSigningKey = true,

// Add your issuer and signing key here

};

    });


services.AddControllers();


    }


public void Configure(IApplicationBuilder app,
IWebHostEnvironment env)

{
```

```
if (env.IsDevelopment())

{

app.UseDeveloperExceptionPage();

}

else

{

app.UseExceptionHandler("/Home/Error");

app.UseHsts();

}


app.UseHttpsRedirection();

app.UseRouting();

app.UseAuthentication();

app.UseAuthorization();

app.UseEndpoints(endpoints =>

{
```

```
endpoints.MapControllers();

});

}
```

Choosing the Right Framework for Your API

Selecting the right framework for your API is crucial and can depend on various factors, including team expertise, project requirements, and the specific use cases of your application. Here are some considerations for choosing between Express.js, Flask, and ASP.NET Core.

1. Project Requirements

1.1 Complexity of the API

Express.js: Ideal for applications requiring flexibility and customization. Use it when you need a lightweight framework to quickly develop RESTful APIs.

Flask: Suitable for simpler applications or microservices. Choose Flask when you need rapid development with minimal overhead.

ASP.NET Core: Best for enterprise-level applications that require robust security, extensive features, and high performance.

2. Team Expertise

2.1 Familiarity with Programming Languages

Express.js: If your team is proficient in JavaScript and familiar with Node.js, Express.js is a natural choice.

Flask: If your team has experience with Python, Flask can be an excellent option for quickly building APIs.

ASP.NET Core: Choose ASP.NET Core if your team is skilled in C# and the .NET ecosystem.

3. Performance and Scalability

3.1 Handling Traffic

Express.js: Can handle high traffic effectively but may require additional optimization and scaling strategies for larger applications.

Flask: Suitable for moderate traffic. When building larger applications, consider using additional libraries for scalability.

ASP.NET Core: Known for high performance and efficiency. It can handle large volumes of traffic, making it ideal for enterprise applications.

4. Community and Ecosystem

4.1 Support and Resources

Express.js: A large community with numerous middleware options and resources available.

Flask: A supportive community with extensive documentation and third-party libraries.

ASP.NET Core: Backed by Microsoft, it has strong community support, extensive documentation, and a wealth of resources for developers.

5. Development Speed

5.1 Rapid Prototyping

Express.js: Enables rapid prototyping with minimal setup, making it a favorite for startups and small projects.

Flask: Designed for quick development cycles, ideal for MVPs (Minimum Viable Products).

ASP.NET Core: While powerful, it may have a steeper learning curve for beginners, which could slow initial development.

Conclusion

In this chapter, we explored real-world API development with popular frameworks such as Express.js, Flask, and ASP.NET Core. We examined the key features of each framework, walked through practical examples of building simple APIs, and discussed factors to consider when choosing the right framework for your needs.

Key Takeaways:

Framework Selection: Choosing the right framework is crucial for the success of your API. Consider project requirements, team expertise, and expected traffic when making your choice.

Security Practices: Implement security best practices, including middleware for authentication and data validation, regardless of the framework used.

Rapid Development: Leverage the strengths of each framework to accelerate development and create efficient APIs.

As you continue your journey in API development, these frameworks offer powerful tools and capabilities that can help you build robust and scalable APIs that meet the needs of your applications and users.

Chapter 14: Building a Complete Full-Stack Application with ASP.NET Core and Angular

I
n today's web development landscape, the ability to create full-stack applications is a highly sought-after skill. Combining the robust capabilities of ASP.NET Core for backend development with the dynamic, user-friendly interface of Angular for frontend development allows developers to build scalable, high-performance web applications. This chapter will guide you through the process of creating a complete full-stack application, providing detailed explanations, code snippets, and best practices along the way.

Understanding the Project Structure (1000 words)

1. Overview of the Application

Before diving into the development process, it's essential to outline the project you will be building. For this chapter, we will create a simple task management application where users can create, read, update, and delete tasks.

Key Features of the Application:

- User authentication and authorization.

- CRUD operations for managing tasks.
- Responsive UI using Angular.
- RESTful API built with ASP.NET Core.

2. Setting Up the Development Environment

To begin, ensure you have the necessary tools installed on your machine:

- **Visual Studio or Visual Studio Code**: IDEs for ASP.NET Core development.
- **Node.js**: Required for Angular development.
- **Angular CLI**: Command-line interface for Angular.
- **SQL Server**: For database management (can also use SQLite for simplicity).

Installing Tools:

- Download and install Visual Studio from the official website.
- Download Node.js from nodejs.org.
- Install Angular CLI globally using npm:

```bash
Copy code
npm install -g @angular/cli
```

3. Creating the Project Structure

Start by creating the backend and frontend projects. Open Visual Studio and create a new ASP.NET Core Web API project.

Creating the ASP.NET Core Project:

1. Launch Visual Studio and select "Create a new project."
2. Choose "ASP.NET Core Web Application" and click "Next."
3. Name your project (e.g., TaskManagementAPI) and select the project

185

location.

4. Choose the API template and ensure you have .NET 6.0 (or the latest version) selected.

Creating the Angular Project: Open your command line interface and navigate to the folder where you want to create the Angular application. Use Angular CLI to create a new project.

```bash
Copy code
ng new task-management-client
```

Follow the prompts to set up your Angular application, choosing routing and styles (CSS, SCSS, etc.) as per your preference.

Setting Up the ASP.NET Core Backend (2000 words)

1. Configuring the Database

We'll use Entity Framework Core for database management. First, add the necessary NuGet packages for Entity Framework Core and SQL Server.

Installing Entity Framework Core Packages: Open the Package Manager Console in Visual Studio and run the following commands:

```powershell
Copy code
Install-Package Microsoft.EntityFrameworkCore.SqlServer
Install-Package Microsoft.EntityFrameworkCore.Tools
```

2. Creating the Data Model

Define a data model for the tasks. Create a new folder named Models in your project and add a TaskItem.cs class.

TaskItem.cs:

```csharp
Copy code
using System.ComponentModel.DataAnnotations;

namespace TaskManagementAPI.Models
{
    public class TaskItem
    {
        [Key]
        public int Id { get; set; }
        public string Title { get; set; }
        public string Description { get; set; }
        public bool IsCompleted { get; set; }
    }
}
```

3. Setting Up the Database Context

Create a Data folder and add a TaskContext.cs file. This context will manage database operations.

TaskContext.cs:

```csharp
Copy code
using Microsoft.EntityFrameworkCore;

namespace TaskManagementAPI.Data
{
    public class TaskContext : DbContext
    {
        public TaskContext(DbContextOptions
<TaskContext> options) : base(options) { }

        public DbSet<TaskItem> TaskItems { get; set; }
    }
}
```

4. Configuring Services and Middleware

In Startup.cs, configure services and middleware to set up the database connection and enable routing.

Startup.cs:

```csharp
Copy code
using Microsoft.EntityFrameworkCore;
using TaskManagementAPI.Data;

public class Startup
{
    public void ConfigureServices
(IServiceCollection services)
    {
        services.AddDbContext<TaskContext>(options =>
            options.UseSqlServer(Configuration.
GetConnectionString("DefaultConnection")));
        services.AddControllers();
    }

    public void Configure(IApplicationBuilder app,
    IWebHostEnvironment env)
    {
        if (env.IsDevelopment())
        {
            app.UseDeveloperExceptionPage();
        }

        app.UseRouting();
        app.UseAuthorization();
        app.UseEndpoints(endpoints =>
        {
            endpoints.MapControllers();
        });
    }
}
```

5. Creating the Task Controller

Create a new folder named Controllers and add a TaskController.cs file to handle API requests.

TaskController.cs:

```csharp
Copy code
using Microsoft.AspNetCore.Mvc;
using Microsoft.EntityFrameworkCore;
using TaskManagementAPI.Data;
using TaskManagementAPI.Models;

namespace TaskManagementAPI.
Controllers
{
[Route("api/[controller]")]
[ApiController]
public class TaskController
: ControllerBase
    {
private readonly
TaskContext _context;

public TaskController
(TaskContext context)
        {
_context = context;
        }

// GET: api/task
[HttpGet]
public async Task<ActionResult
<IEnumerable<TaskItem>>> GetTasks()
        {
return await _context.
TaskItems.ToListAsync();
        }

// POST: api/task
[HttpPost]
public async Task<ActionResult
<TaskItem>> PostTask
(TaskItem taskItem)
        {
_context.TaskItems.
```

```
Add(taskItem);
await _context.
SaveChangesAsync();
return CreatedAtAction
("GetTask", new
{ id = taskItem.Id },
taskItem);
        }


// Additional methods for
PUT and DELETE go here
      }
}
```

6. Configuring the Database Connection

In appsettings.json, configure the connection string for your SQL Server database.

appsettings.json:

```json
Copy code
{
   "ConnectionStrings": {
"DefaultConnection": "Server=your
_server_name;Database=
TaskManagementDB;
Trusted_Connection=True;"
   },
   "Logging": {
"LogLevel": {
"Default": "Information",
"Microsoft": "Warning",
"Microsoft.Hosting.
Lifetime": "Information"
     }
   },
   "AllowedHosts": "*"
}
```

Replace your_server_name with your actual SQL Server instance name.

7. Applying Migrations

To create the database schema based on your data model, use Entity Framework Core migrations.

1. Open the Package Manager Console.
2. Run the following commands:

```powershell
Copy code
Add-Migration InitialCreate
Update-Database
```

This will create the initial migration and update the database to reflect the changes.

Setting Up the Angular Frontend (2000 words)

1. Setting Up Angular Routing

First, set up routing in your Angular application. Open app-routing.module.ts and configure your routes.

app-routing.module.ts:

```typescript
Copy code
import { NgModule } from '@angular/core';
import { RouterModule, Routes } from
'@angular/router';
import { TaskListComponent } from '.
/task-list/task-list.component';
import { TaskDetailComponent } from
'./task-detail/task-detail.component';

const routes: Routes = [
```

```
  { path: '', redirectTo:
'/tasks', pathMatch: 'full' },
  { path: 'tasks', component:
TaskListComponent },
  { path: 'tasks/:id',
 component: TaskDetailComponent },
];

@NgModule({
  imports: [RouterModule.
forRoot(routes)],
  exports: [RouterModule]
})
export class AppRoutingModule { }
```

2. Creating Components

Next, create the necessary components for the task management application.

1. **Task List Component**: This component will display a list of tasks.

```bash
Copy code
ng generate component task-list
```

1. **Task Detail Component**: This component will display details of a single task.

```bash
Copy code
ng generate component task-detail
```

3. Building the Task Service

Create a service to handle HTTP requests to the ASP.NET Core backend.

1. Generate a service:

```bash
Copy code
ng generate service task
```

1. Implement the service methods to interact with the API.

task.service.ts:

```typescript
Copy code
import { Injectable } from
'@angular/core';
import { HttpClient } from
'@angular/common/http';
import { Observable } from
'rxjs';
import { TaskItem } from '.
/task-item.model';

@Injectable({
  providedIn: 'root'
})
export class TaskService {
  private apiUrl = 'https:
//localhost:5001/api/task';

  constructor(private http:
HttpClient) { }
```

```
getTasks(): Observable<TaskItem[]> {
    return this.http.get<
TaskItem[]>(this.apiUrl);
  }

  getTask(id: number):
Observable<TaskItem> {
    return this.http.get<TaskItem>
(`${this.apiUrl}/${id}`);
  }

  addTask(task: TaskItem):
Observable<TaskItem> {
    return this.http.post
<TaskItem>(this.apiUrl, task);
  }

  updateTask(task: TaskItem):
Observable<TaskItem> {
    return this.http.put<TaskItem>
(`${this.apiUrl}/${task.id}`, task);
  }

  deleteTask(id: number): Observable<void> {
    return this.http.delete<void>
(`${this.apiUrl}/${id}`);
  }
}
```

4. Implementing the Task List Component

Update the task-list.component.ts to retrieve and display tasks.

task-list.component.ts:

```typescript
Copy code
import { Component, OnInit }
from '@angular/core';
import { TaskService } from
```

```
'../task.service';
import { TaskItem } from
'../task-item.model';

@Component({
  selector: 'app-task-list',
  templateUrl: '.
/task-list.component.html',
  styleUrls: ['.
/task-list.component.css']
})
export class TaskListComponent
implements OnInit {
  tasks: TaskItem[] = [];

  constructor(private taskService:
TaskService) { }

  ngOnInit(): void {
    this.loadTasks();
  }

  loadTasks(): void {
    this.taskService.getTasks().
subscribe(tasks => this.tasks = tasks);
  }
}
```

5. Implementing the Task Detail Component

Update the task-detail.component.ts to handle the display and editing of a single task.

task-detail.component.ts:

```
typescript
Copy code
import { Component, OnInit } from
'@angular/core';
import { ActivatedRoute } from
```

```typescript
'@angular/router';
import { TaskService } from
'../task.service';
import { TaskItem } from
'../task-item.model';

@Component({
selector: 'app-task-detail',
templateUrl: './
task-detail.component.html',
styleUrls: ['./
task-detail.component.css']
})
export class TaskDetailComponent
implements OnInit {
  task: TaskItem | undefined;

  constructor(private route:
 ActivatedRoute, private taskService:
 TaskService) { }

  ngOnInit(): void {
    const id = +this.route.snapshot.
paramMap.get('id')!;
    this.taskService.getTask(id).
subscribe(task => this.task = task);
  }
}
```

6. Configuring Angular HTTP Client

To enable HTTP requests, import the HttpClientModule in your app.module.ts.

app.module.ts:

```typescript
typescript
Copy code
import { HttpClientModule } from '@angular/common/http';
```

```
@NgModule({
  declarations: [
    // Your components
  ],
  imports: [
    HttpClientModule,
    AppRoutingModule,
    // Other modules
  ],
  providers: [],
  bootstrap: [AppComponent]
})
export class AppModule { }
```

Connecting the Frontend and Backend (1000 words)

1. CORS Configuration in ASP.NET Core

To allow your Angular application to communicate with the ASP.NET Core API, configure Cross-Origin Resource Sharing (CORS) in your backend.

Configuring CORS: In Startup.cs, add the following lines in the Config-ureServices method:

```
csharp
Copy code
public void ConfigureServices
(IServiceCollection services)
{
services.AddCors(options =>
    {
options.AddPolicy("AllowAllOrigins",
builder => builder.
AllowAnyOrigin().
AllowAnyMethod().AllowAnyHeader());
    });

    services.AddDbContext
```

```
<TaskContext>(options =>
options.UseSqlServer(Configuration.
GetConnectionString
("DefaultConnection")));
services.AddControllers();
}
```

Then, in the Configure method, enable the CORS policy:

```csharp
Copy code
public void Configure
(IApplicationBuilder app,
IWebHostEnvironment env)
{
if (env.IsDevelopment())
    {
app.UseDeveloperExceptionPage();
    }

app.UseRouting();
app.UseCors("AllowAllOrigins");
app.UseAuthorization();
app.UseEndpoints(endpoints =>
    {
endpoints.MapControllers();
    });
}
```

2. Testing the API with Postman

Before testing the Angular frontend, ensure that your API is functioning correctly. Use Postman to test the CRUD operations.

- **GET Tasks**: Send a GET request to https://localhost:5001/api/task.
- **POST Task**: Use a POST request to create a new task with a JSON body.
- **PUT Task**: Update a task using a PUT request with the task ID.
- **DELETE Task**: Delete a task using a DELETE request with the task ID.

3. Running the Angular Application

Once you confirm the API is working correctly, run your Angular application. Navigate to your Angular project folder and use the following command:

```bash
Copy code
ng serve
```

Your application will be available at http://localhost:4200. Test the frontend to ensure it interacts correctly with the backend API.

Deploying the Full-Stack Application (1000 words)

1. Preparing the ASP.NET Core Application for Deployment

To deploy your ASP.NET Core application, follow these steps:

- **Publish the Application**: Use Visual Studio to publish your application. Right-click on the project in Solution Explorer, select "Publish," and follow the prompts to create a publish profile.
- **Choose Hosting Environment**: You can deploy to various environments such as Azure, AWS, or any hosting provider that supports .NET applications. For Azure, use Azure App Service for easy deployment.

2. Deploying the Angular Application

To deploy your Angular application, you need to build it for production.

- **Build the Application**: Run the following command in your Angular project folder:

```bash
bash
Copy code
ng build --prod
```

- **Deploy the Build**: The build artifacts will be located in the dist folder. You can deploy these files to a web server, such as Nginx or Apache, or use cloud platforms like Firebase Hosting or Azure Static Web Apps.

3. Configuring the Server

Once deployed, ensure your server is configured correctly to serve both the API and the Angular frontend.

- **Serve Static Files**: If using ASP.NET Core to serve the Angular frontend, configure the middleware to serve static files from the dist folder.

Example Configuration:

```csharp
csharp
Copy code
app.UseStaticFiles();
app.UseRouting();
app.UseEndpoints(endpoints =>
{
    endpoints.MapControllers();
    endpoints.MapFallbackToFile
("index.html"); // Serve Angular app
});
```

Conclusion

In this chapter, we have explored the process of building a complete full-stack application using ASP.NET Core for the backend and Angular for the frontend. We started by understanding the project structure and setting up the development environment, then moved on to creating the backend API, implementing the Angular frontend, and finally deploying the application.

Building a full-stack application is a rewarding experience that allows you to leverage the strengths of both ASP.NET Core and Angular, enabling you to create powerful, interactive web applications. As you continue to develop your skills, remember that the journey of learning and growth never ends. Embrace new challenges, explore advanced concepts, and stay curious as you build your expertise in full-stack development.

Chapter 15: Common API Development Pitfalls and How to Avoid Them

Building APIs can be an incredibly rewarding endeavor, allowing developers to create powerful integrations and enhance user experiences. However, it can also be fraught with challenges. Beginners and experienced developers alike can fall into common traps that lead to ineffective, confusing, or unusable APIs. In this chapter, we will explore these pitfalls, providing insights and strategies to help you avoid them. By learning from the mistakes of others and understanding the best practices for API development, you can create robust, user-friendly APIs that stand the test of time.

Mistakes Beginners Make When Designing APIs

1. Lack of Clear Purpose and Scope

One of the most significant mistakes beginners make when designing APIs is failing to define a clear purpose and scope. An API should have a specific function that solves a particular problem or provides a distinct service.

- **Understanding User Needs**: Before designing an API, it's crucial to understand the needs of its intended users. Failing to gather requirements can lead to features that are unnecessary or misaligned with user expectations.

- **Example**: Consider an API designed to manage user accounts. Without a clear purpose, the API might include redundant features or miss essential functionalities, such as user authentication or profile management.

Solution:

- **Define Objectives**: Start by defining the objectives of your API. What problem does it solve? Who will use it? What features are necessary? Engaging with potential users and stakeholders during this phase can provide valuable insights.
- **Create a Requirements Document**: Develop a requirements document outlining the API's purpose, key functionalities, and user stories. This document serves as a roadmap for the design and development process.

2. Poorly Designed Endpoints

Another common mistake is creating poorly designed endpoints. API endpoints should be intuitive, predictable, and follow established conventions to make them easy to use.

- **Inconsistent Naming Conventions**: Inconsistent naming conventions can confuse developers. For example, using different terms for similar resources across endpoints can lead to misunderstandings.
- **Example**: An API that manages tasks might have endpoints like /create-task, /tasks, and /removeTask. The inconsistency in naming makes it harder for developers to remember and understand the API.

Solution:

- **Follow RESTful Principles**: Design endpoints according to RESTful principles. Use nouns for resources and standard HTTP methods

(GET, POST, PUT, DELETE) to perform actions on those resources. For example, use /tasks to represent task resources and employ the appropriate HTTP methods for CRUD operations.

- **Use Consistent Naming**: Establish a consistent naming convention for your endpoints and stick to it throughout the API. This consistency enhances usability and makes the API more intuitive.

3. Inadequate Error Handling

Inadequate error handling is a common pitfall that can lead to frustration for developers using your API. When errors occur, the API should provide clear and actionable feedback.

- **Vague Error Messages**: Providing vague error messages that lack context can make troubleshooting difficult. Developers need specific information to diagnose and resolve issues.
- **Example**: An API that returns a generic error message like "An error occurred" does not provide enough information for the developer to identify the problem.

Solution:

- **Define Standard Error Responses**: Create a standardized error response format that includes meaningful information. Include fields such as error codes, messages, and details about the issue.
- **Use HTTP Status Codes Appropriately**: Utilize appropriate HTTP status codes to indicate the success or failure of requests. For example, use 404 for "Not Found," 401 for "Unauthorized," and 400 for "Bad Request." This helps developers understand the nature of the error.

4. Lack of Versioning

Failing to implement versioning can create significant challenges as your API evolves. Without versioning, changes to the API can break existing integrations, leading to frustration for users.

- **Example**: An API that adds a new required parameter to an endpoint without versioning can cause existing applications to fail if they do not accommodate the change.

Solution:

- **Implement Versioning Early**: Incorporate versioning into your API from the beginning. Use URL-based versioning (e.g., /v1/tasks) or header-based versioning to specify the API version. This approach allows you to make changes without disrupting existing users.
- **Communicate Changes**: Clearly communicate any changes or deprecations in your API. Provide a migration guide to help users transition to new versions smoothly.

5. Neglecting Documentation

Neglecting to provide thorough documentation is a frequent mistake that can hinder adoption and usability. Comprehensive documentation is essential for developers to understand how to use your API effectively.

- **Example**: An API without proper documentation may lead to confusion and frustration, causing developers to abandon it in favor of better-documented alternatives.

Solution:

- **Create Comprehensive Documentation**: Invest time in creating clear and detailed documentation for your API. Include endpoint descriptions, request and response examples, authentication details, and error codes.

- **Use Tools for Documentation**: Leverage tools like Swagger or Postman to generate interactive documentation. These tools enhance usability and make it easier for developers to explore the API.

How to Manage Dependencies and Third-Party APIs

1. Understanding Dependencies

Managing dependencies and third-party APIs is a critical aspect of API development. Dependencies can introduce complexity, increase the risk of failure, and impact the stability of your application.

- **Assessing Dependencies**: Before integrating third-party APIs or libraries, assess their reliability, security, and performance. Evaluate whether they align with your project's requirements and long-term goals.
- **Example**: Integrating a payment processing API without thorough evaluation may expose your application to security vulnerabilities or service disruptions if the API experiences downtime.

Solution:

- **Choose Reliable Partners**: Select reputable and well-supported third-party APIs. Research their track record, user reviews, and documentation to ensure reliability.
- **Monitor Dependencies**: Regularly monitor the health and performance of third-party APIs. Use tools and services that alert you to changes or issues with your dependencies.

2. Version Compatibility

When using third-party APIs, version compatibility is crucial. Changes in the third-party API can affect your application's functionality, leading to potential failures.

- **Example**: A third-party library may release a new version that breaks backward compatibility, resulting in errors in your application.

Solution:

- **Pin Versions**: If applicable, pin your dependencies to specific versions in your package management system. This approach helps avoid unexpected breaking changes.
- **Regular Updates**: Regularly review and update your dependencies to ensure compatibility and security. Establish a process for testing updates in a staging environment before deploying them to production.

3. Error Handling with Third-Party APIs

When working with third-party APIs, robust error handling is essential. External APIs may experience downtime or unexpected behavior that can affect your application.

- **Example**: If a third-party API fails to respond, your application should handle the error gracefully and provide meaningful feedback to users.

Solution:

- **Implement Retry Logic**: Consider implementing retry logic for transient errors, such as network timeouts. Use exponential backoff strategies to avoid overwhelming the third-party API.
- **Fallback Mechanisms**: Develop fallback mechanisms to ensure your

application remains functional if the third-party API is unavailable. For example, cache previous responses or provide alternative services.

4. Security Considerations

Integrating third-party APIs raises important security considerations. Protecting sensitive data and ensuring secure communication is paramount.

- **Example**: Failing to secure API keys or sensitive information when communicating with third-party APIs can lead to data breaches or unauthorized access.

Solution:

- **Use Secure Communication**: Always use HTTPS for secure communication with third-party APIs. Ensure that sensitive data, such as API keys and user credentials, is transmitted securely.
- **Secure Storage**: Store sensitive information securely. Use environment variables or secret management tools to keep API keys and tokens confidential.

Avoiding Over-Engineering and Over-Complication

1. Understanding Over-Engineering

Over-engineering occurs when developers add unnecessary complexity to an API, making it harder to use and maintain. This can stem from a desire to anticipate every possible use case or accommodate future requirements that may never materialize.

- **Example**: An API designed to manage user accounts may include excessive features like role-based access control, detailed logging, and complex validation that complicates its primary function.

Solution:

- **Focus on Core Functionality**: Prioritize the core functionality of your API. Define the primary use cases and build around them, avoiding unnecessary features that may complicate the design.
- **Iterative Development**: Adopt an iterative development approach. Start with a minimum viable product (MVP) that addresses essential user needs, then gather feedback to refine and expand features as necessary.

2. Striving for Simplicity

Simplicity is a key principle in API design. A simple, intuitive API is easier for developers to understand and integrate.

- **Example**: An API with a convoluted structure, unclear endpoints, and unnecessary parameters will frustrate developers and hinder adoption.

Solution:

- **Simplify Endpoints**: Use straightforward endpoint designs and consistent naming conventions. Ensure that each endpoint serves a specific purpose and is easy to remember.
- **Clear Documentation**: Provide clear and concise documentation that explains how to use the API without overwhelming developers with unnecessary information.

3. Avoiding Premature Optimization

Premature optimization is the practice of optimizing code or design before there is a real need for it. This can lead to complexity without tangible benefits.

- **Example**: Spending excessive time optimizing an API for performance without evidence that it is a bottleneck can divert resources from more pressing issues.

Solution:

- **Focus on Readability**: Prioritize code readability and maintainability over premature optimization. Optimize only when there is clear evidence of performance issues.
- **Measure Performance**: Use monitoring tools to measure API performance and identify bottlenecks. This data-driven approach enables you to make informed decisions about where optimization efforts are needed.

4. Regularly Review and Refactor

Regularly reviewing and refactoring your API can help identify areas of complexity that need simplification. This practice ensures that the API remains maintainable and user-friendly.

- **Example**: An API that has evolved over time may accumulate unnecessary features or complex logic, making it harder to manage.

Solution:

- **Conduct Code Reviews**: Implement a code review process to identify complexity and maintainability issues. Encourage team members to provide constructive feedback on API design.
- **Plan for Refactoring**: Allocate time for regular refactoring sessions to simplify the codebase, remove unnecessary features, and improve overall design.

Learning from API Failures and Real-World Case Studies

1. Analyzing API Failures

Learning from the failures of other APIs can provide valuable insights into what to avoid in your development process. Analyzing real-world case studies helps identify common pitfalls and best practices.

- **Example**: The Twitter API faced significant challenges during its early years, struggling with rate limits and API stability. Developers often encountered frustrating error messages and inconsistent behavior.

Key Takeaways from Twitter API Failure:

- **Implement Robust Rate Limiting**: Ensure that your API has a well-defined rate limiting strategy to prevent abuse and ensure stability.
- **Provide Meaningful Error Messages**: Clear error messages help developers troubleshoot issues and enhance the user experience.

2. Case Study: Dropbox API

The Dropbox API is a great example of successful API design. Dropbox focused on creating a user-friendly API that developers could easily integrate into their applications.

Key Features of the Dropbox API:

- **Clear Documentation**: Dropbox provides extensive documentation that is easy to navigate, with clear examples and explanations of features.
- **Simplicity and Usability**: The API design is intuitive, allowing developers to quickly access core functionalities like file uploads, sharing, and metadata retrieval.

Lessons Learned from Dropbox:

- **Prioritize Documentation**: Comprehensive and user-friendly documentation can significantly enhance the developer experience and drive adoption.

- **Focus on User Needs**: Understanding the needs of your users and building the API around those needs fosters a more effective and usable API.

3. Case Study: Twilio API

The Twilio API has gained widespread adoption due to its straightforward design and developer-centric approach. Twilio focuses on providing clear functionalities for communication services such as SMS, voice, and video.

Key Features of the Twilio API:

- **Clear and Concise Documentation**: Twilio's documentation is easy to follow, with well-organized sections and interactive examples.
- **Developer Support**: Twilio offers robust support channels, including forums, tutorials, and customer support, ensuring that developers can get help when needed.

Lessons Learned from Twilio:

- **Provide Excellent Support**: Offering strong support channels enhances the developer experience and builds trust with your users.
- **Create an Engaging Developer Community**: Encouraging community engagement fosters a sense of belonging and helps developers learn from each other.

Conclusion

In this chapter, we explored common API development pitfalls and provided insights on how to avoid them. From mistakes that beginners often make when designing APIs to managing dependencies, avoiding over-engineering, and learning from real-world failures, the key to successful API development lies in careful planning, user-centric design, and a commitment to continuous improvement.

By understanding the importance of clear purpose, intuitive design, and robust documentation, you can create APIs that foster developer adoption and engagement. Remember that the journey of API development is ongoing, and learning from both successes and failures will pave the way for creating powerful, user-friendly APIs.

As you move forward in your API development journey, keep these lessons in mind. By prioritizing the needs of your users, investing in clear documentation, and maintaining a commitment to excellence, you will be well on your way to building APIs that developers love to use.

Conclusion: Your Journey Beyond API Development

As we conclude this exploration of API development, it's essential to reflect on the key concepts and practices we've covered throughout this book. API development is a multifaceted discipline that requires a combination of technical skills, thoughtful design, and a commitment to creating user-friendly solutions. This conclusion will summarize these concepts, discuss advanced topics and next steps for your learning journey, provide resources for further mastery, and offer final thoughts on building better APIs.

Recap of Key Concepts and Practices

Throughout this book, we delved into various aspects of API development, emphasizing the importance of thoughtful design, comprehensive documentation, and effective communication with users. Here are some of the key concepts and practices we've discussed:

1. Importance of Planning and Design

Effective API development begins with careful planning and design. Understanding the purpose of your API, the needs of its users, and the functionality it will provide is crucial. We explored:

- **Defining Objectives**: Before coding, it's vital to define clear objectives and requirements for your API. Engaging with potential users during this phase ensures the API addresses their needs.
- **RESTful Principles**: Following RESTful principles promotes a clean and intuitive API design. Use consistent naming conventions, logical endpoint structures, and standard HTTP methods to create a user-friendly experience.

2. Clear and Comprehensive Documentation

We emphasized the role of documentation as the backbone of successful API adoption. Comprehensive documentation not only helps developers understand how to use the API but also fosters a positive developer experience. Key points included:

- **Structured Format**: Organize your documentation into clear sections, such as overview, authentication, endpoints, and error handling. This structure enhances usability and helps developers quickly find the information they need.
- **Code Examples**: Including clear, relevant code examples demonstrates practical usage and helps users implement the API more effectively.

3. Error Handling and Versioning

Robust error handling and effective versioning strategies are essential for maintaining an API that evolves over time. We discussed:

- **Standardized Error Responses**: Provide meaningful error messages and utilize appropriate HTTP status codes to help developers diagnose issues quickly.
- **Implementing Versioning**: Versioning your API from the outset ensures that changes can be made without disrupting existing users, making it easier to introduce new features and improvements.

4. Avoiding Common Pitfalls

We explored common pitfalls that API developers encounter, such as lack of clear purpose, poorly designed endpoints, inadequate error handling, and neglecting documentation. We discussed strategies to avoid these pitfalls:

- **User-Centric Design**: Prioritize the needs of your users when designing your API. Engage with developers to gather feedback and iterate on the design.
- **Simplicity and Clarity**: Aim for simplicity in your API design and documentation. Avoid over-engineering and ensure that the API remains intuitive and easy to use.

5. Learning from Real-World Case Studies

Throughout the book, we analyzed real-world case studies of successful and failed APIs. These examples provided valuable insights into best practices and potential pitfalls. Key takeaways included:

- **The Importance of Support**: APIs like Twilio, which provide excellent support and documentation, foster a thriving developer community and drive adoption.
- **Learning from Failures**: Understanding the failures of APIs, such as the Twitter API's early struggles, offers crucial lessons in rate limiting, error messaging, and the need for robust documentation.

Where to Go from Here: Advanced Topics and Next Steps

Having laid the groundwork for effective API development, it's time to explore advanced topics and next steps in your learning journey. Here are some areas you might consider delving into:

1. API Security

As APIs become more integral to applications, security is paramount. Understanding how to secure your API from potential threats is crucial. Topics to explore include:

- **Authentication and Authorization**: Learn about OAuth2, JWT, and other authentication methods to secure your API.
- **Rate Limiting and Throttling**: Implement strategies to protect your API from abuse and ensure fair usage among users.

2. API Testing and Monitoring

Ensuring the reliability and performance of your API is essential for maintaining user satisfaction. Investigate:

- **Automated Testing**: Explore tools for automated testing of your API, such as Postman, JUnit, or Mocha. Automated tests can help catch issues early and ensure functionality remains intact.
- **Monitoring and Analytics**: Learn how to monitor your API's performance using tools like New Relic or Prometheus. Gathering analytics on API usage can provide insights into user behavior and potential areas for improvement.

3. Building APIs with Microservices

Microservices architecture is gaining popularity for building scalable and maintainable applications. Consider learning about:

- **Microservices Principles**: Understand the principles of microservices and how they differ from traditional monolithic architectures.
- **Service Communication**: Explore methods for communication between microservices, such as REST, gRPC, and message queues.

4. API Design Patterns

Familiarizing yourself with design patterns can enhance your API development skills. Consider studying:

- **GraphQL**: Explore GraphQL as an alternative to REST for building APIs. Learn about its advantages in terms of flexibility and efficiency.
- **Event-Driven APIs**: Investigate event-driven architecture and how it can improve responsiveness and scalability.

Resources for Further Learning and Mastery

To continue your journey in API development, here are some valuable resources that can aid your learning:

1. Books

- **"RESTful Web APIs" by Leonard Richardson and Sam Ruby**: This book provides a comprehensive understanding of RESTful design principles.
- **"API Design Patterns" by JJ Geewax**: This book explores common design patterns used in API development, providing practical examples and best practices.

2. Online Courses

- **Udemy**: Offers a variety of courses on API development, RESTful services, and security.
- **Coursera**: Provides courses from leading universities and institutions on topics such as microservices and API design.

3. Documentation and Blogs

- **API documentation platforms**: Refer to the documentation of well-known APIs like Stripe, Twilio, and GitHub to see best practices in action.
- **Developer blogs**: Follow industry blogs and newsletters, such as those from ProgrammableWeb or the API Evangelist, for the latest trends and insights.

4. Community and Forums

- **Stack Overflow**: Engage with the developer community on platforms like Stack Overflow to ask questions, share knowledge, and learn from others.
- **GitHub**: Explore open-source projects related to API development and contribute to discussions within those communities.

Final Thoughts on Building Better APIs

As you conclude this journey through API development, remember that building effective APIs is both an art and a science. The skills and insights you've gained will serve as a strong foundation for creating APIs that meet the needs of users while promoting adoption and engagement.

Here are some final thoughts to keep in mind as you move forward:

- **Embrace User Feedback**: Always be open to feedback from users and developers. Iterating on your API based on real-world usage can lead to significant improvements and enhancements.

- **Stay Informed and Adaptable**: The tech landscape is constantly evolving, and so are best practices in API development. Stay informed about new technologies, methodologies, and trends to remain competitive in your field.
- **Foster a Growth Mindset**: Approach challenges with curiosity and a willingness to learn. Each obstacle is an opportunity for growth and development.
- **Prioritize Community Building**: Engaging with the developer community can provide support, inspiration, and collaboration opportunities. Contributing to open-source projects or sharing your experiences can create a positive impact.

In conclusion, API development is a dynamic field that offers endless opportunities for innovation and improvement. By applying the principles and practices discussed in this book, you will be well-equipped to design, build, and maintain APIs that stand the test of time and meet the evolving needs of developers and users alike. Your journey is just beginning, and the possibilities are limitless. Embrace the adventure, and continue to build better APIs for a brighter digital future.

www.ingramcontent.com/pod-product-compliance
Lightning Source LLC
LaVergne TN
LVHW051324050326
832903LV00031B/3343